Southern Gospel Piano

Giving Thanks

Darrell Archer

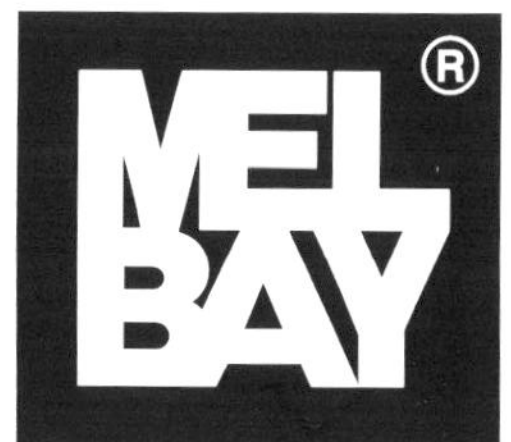

WWW.MELBAY.COM

Preface

As the old saying goes, we all need to have an "attitude of gratitude" for every blessing and gift that comes our way. However, thankfulness cannot be genuinely expressed unless we have a deep awareness of the kindness and love shown by the God to whom we are thankful as the source of all our blessings. Part of our purpose as "We Gather Together," is not only to worship our great God for who he is, but also to express our heartfelt thanks and appreciation for the multitude of gracious gifts that are so abundantly provided to us each day, and which we sometimes take for granted.

So, "Come Ye Thankful People, Come," "Count Your Blessings," and "Rejoice Ye Pure in Heart." "Now Thank We All Our God" for "All Things Bright and Beautiful" and "Let the Whole Creation Cry" in exuberant praise to the lord of all creation. If we do so from our innermost beings, then we can truly say "Brethren, We Have Met to Worship."

This piano collection is made up of southern gospel arrangements of some favorite songs of gratitude and thanksgiving. It is presented in the hope and expectation that those who perform these pieces, as well as those who may hear them, may be instilled with an ever increasing sense of our God's majesty and his goodness unto us.

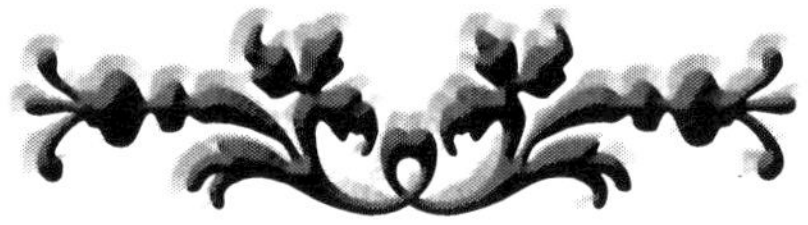

Table of Contents

All Things Bright And Beautiful

William H. Monk
Arr. Darrell V. Archer

Cecil Frances Alexander

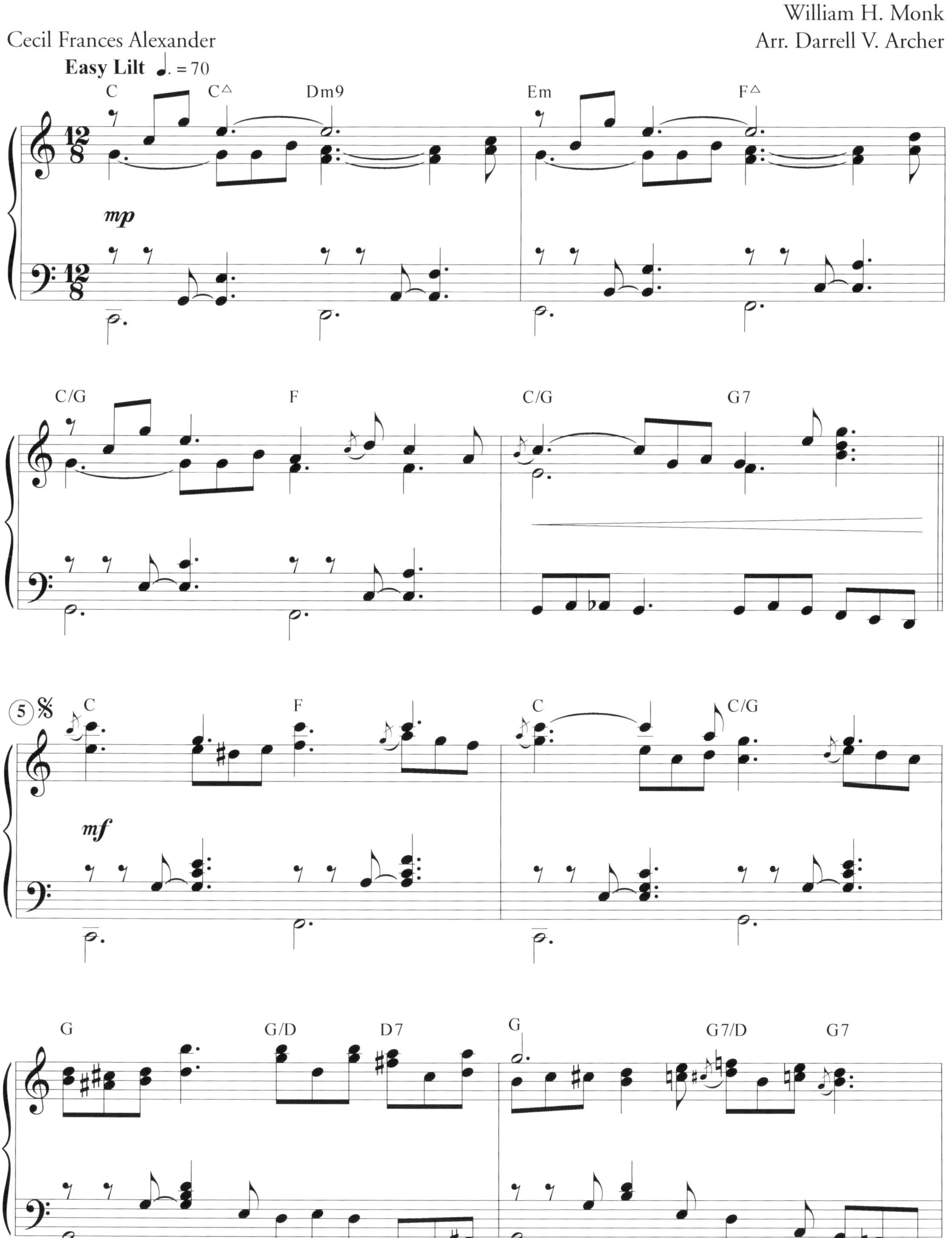

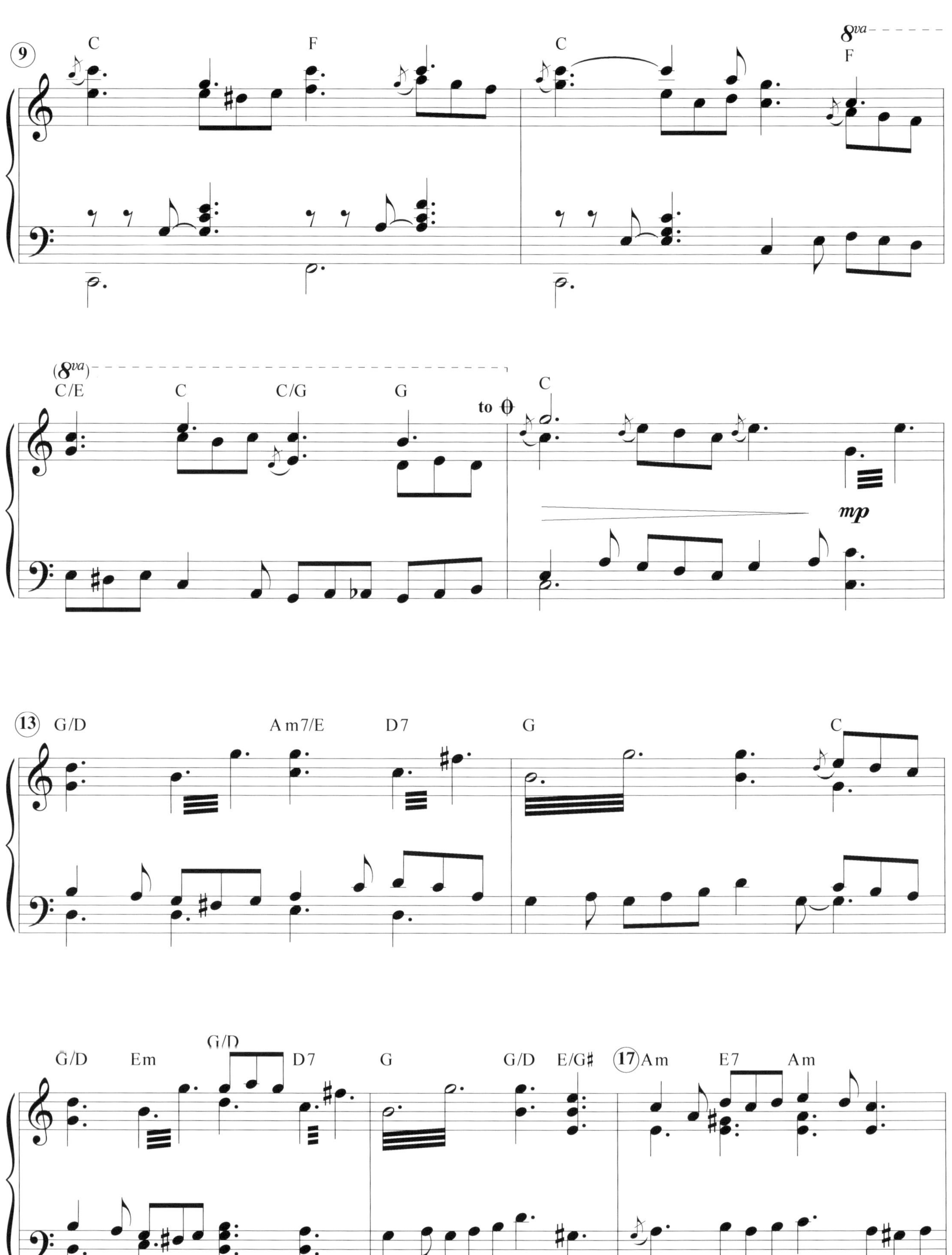

9
C
F
C
8va
F
(8va)
C/E
C
C/G
G
to
C
mp
13
G/D
Am7/E
D7
G
C
G/D
Em
G/D
D7
G
G/D
E/G♯
17
Am
E7
Am

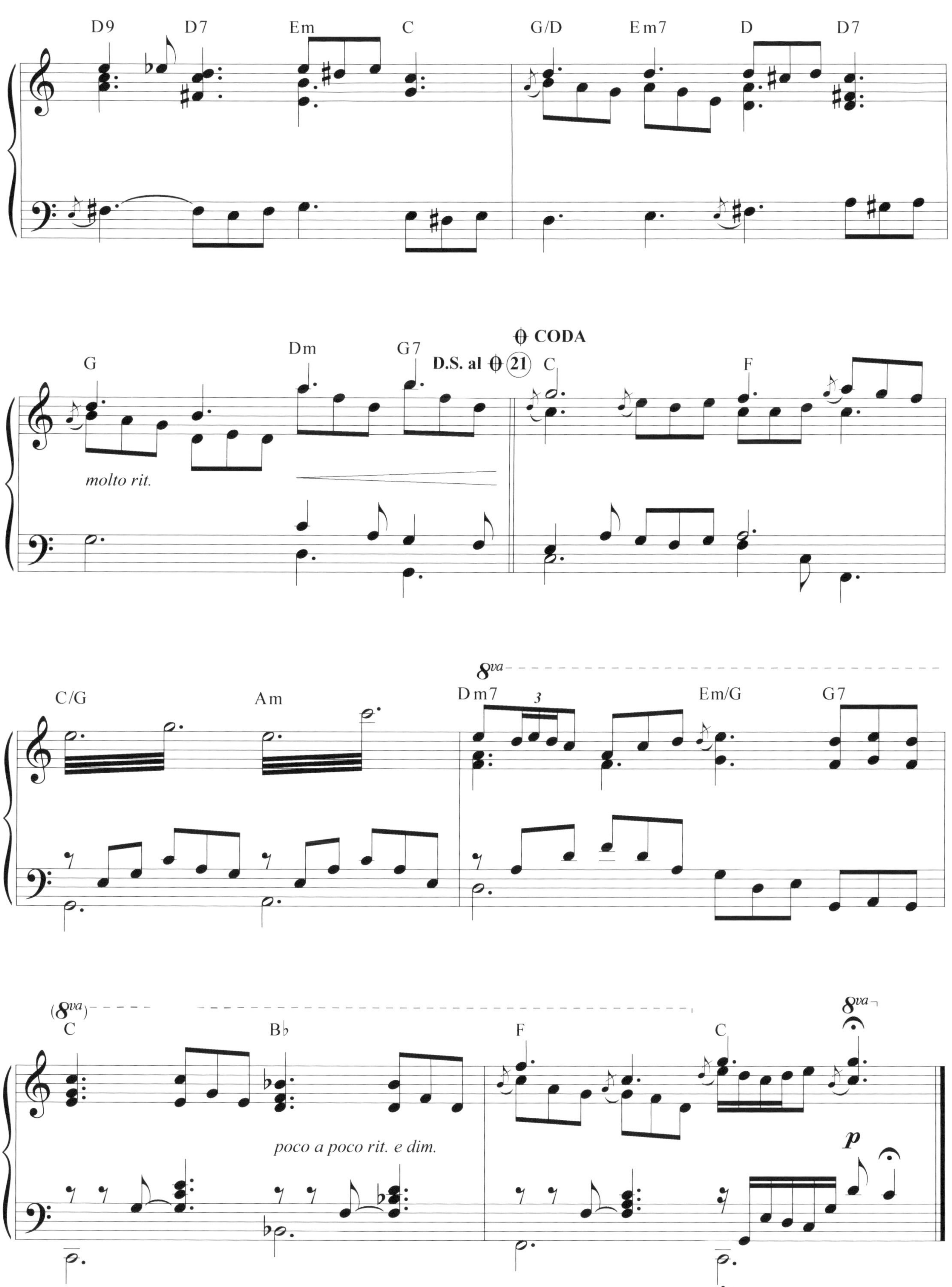
D9
D7
Em
C
G/D
Em7
D
D7
G
Dm
G7
D.S. al 𝄌 21
𝄌 CODA
C
F
molto rit.
C/G
Am
8va
Dm7
3
Em/G
G7
(8va)
C
B♭
F
C
8va
poco a poco rit. e dim.
p

Another Year Is Dawning

Horatius Bonar

Traditional Greek Melody
Arr. Darrell V. Archer

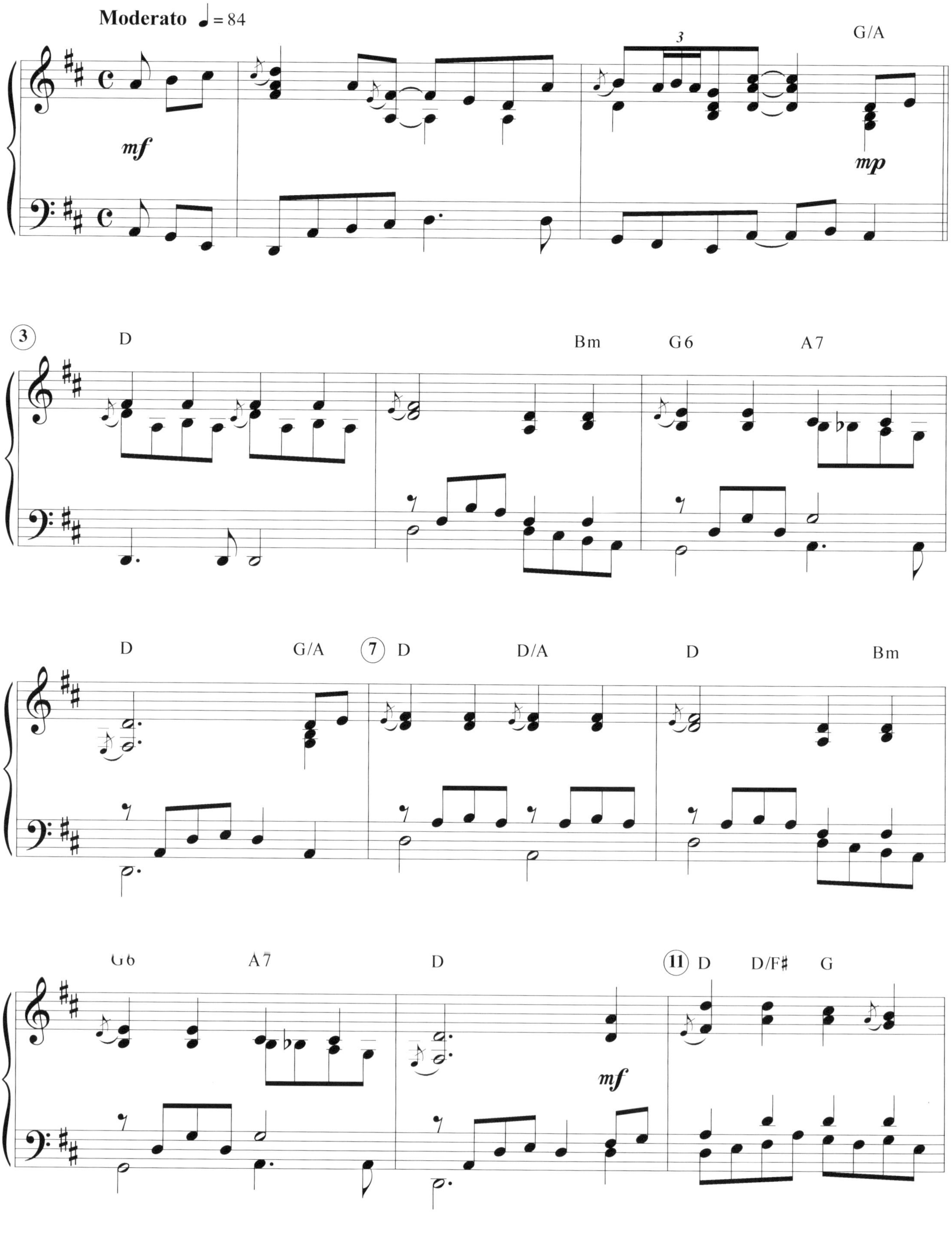

Moderato ♩ = 84

mf

3

G/A

mp

③ D Bm G6 A7

D G/A ⑦ D D/A D Bm

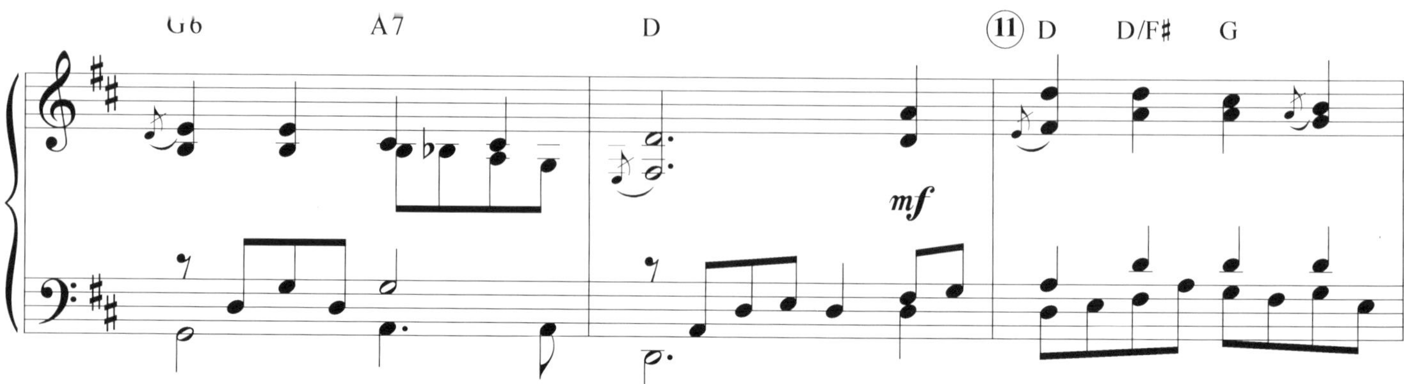

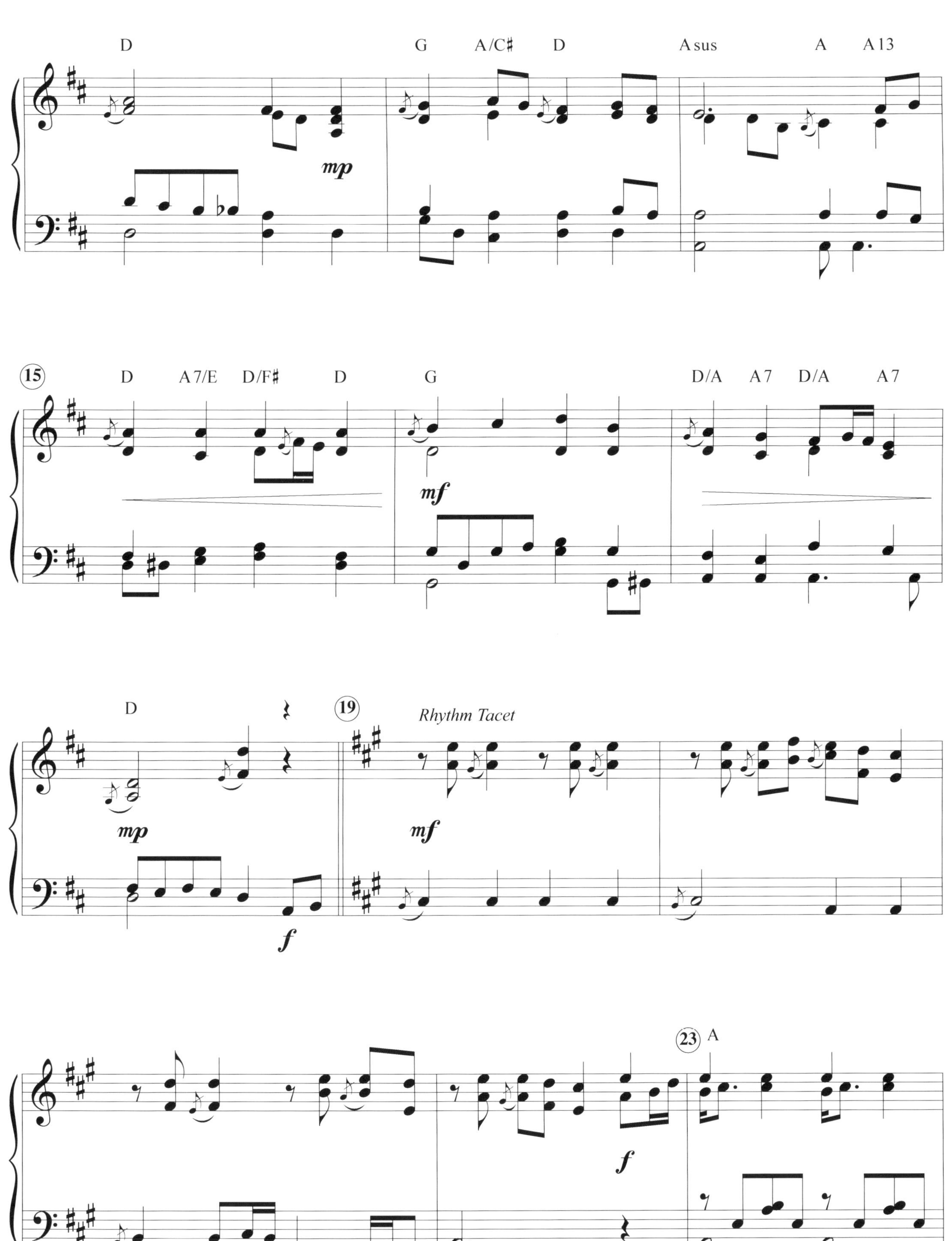
D
G
A/C♯
D
Asus
A
A13
mp
15
D
A7/E
D/F♯
D
G
D/A
A7
D/A
A7
mf
D
19
Rhythm Tacet
mp
mf
f
23
A
f

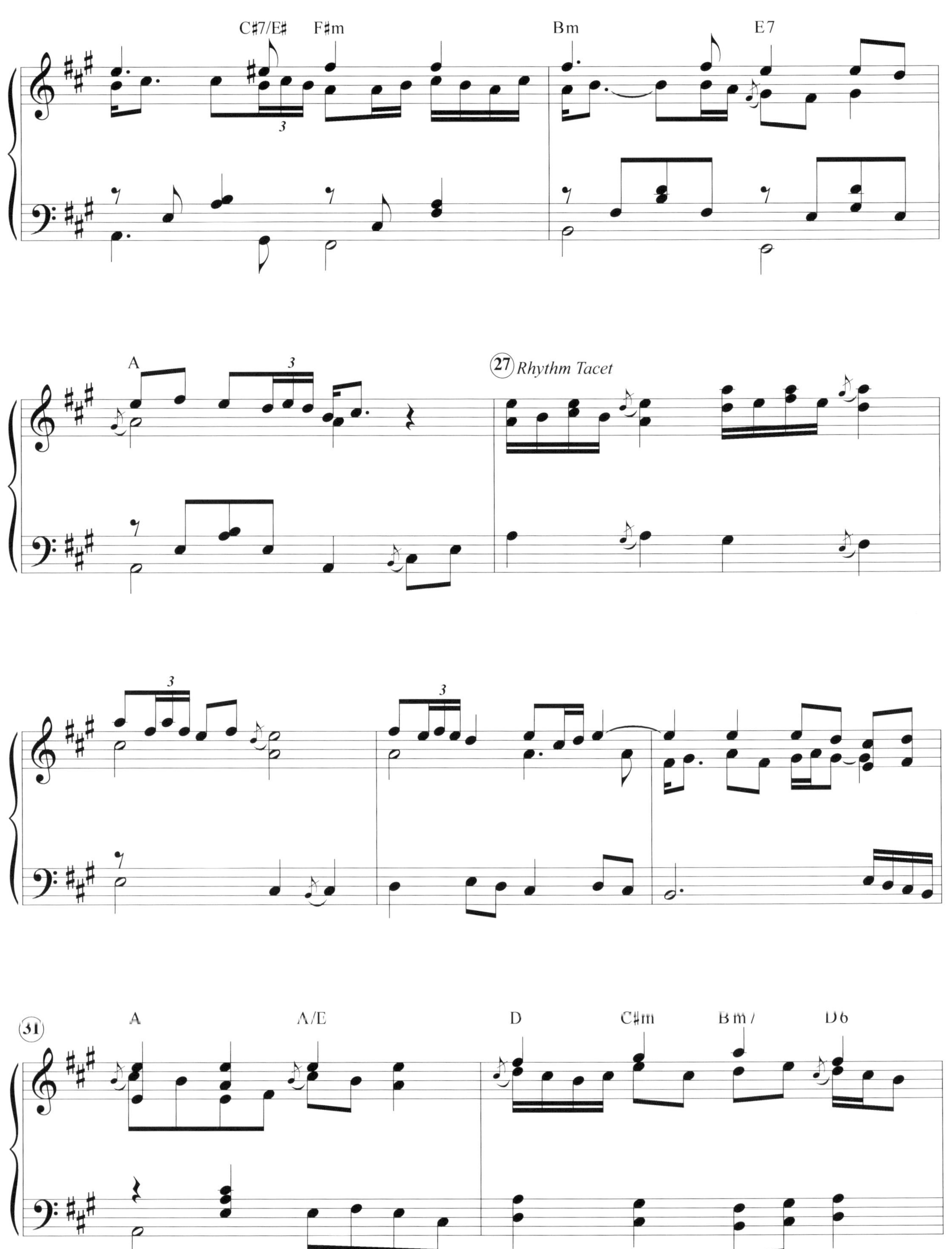
C♯7/E♯
F♯m
Bm
E7
A
27 Rhythm Tacet
3
31
A
A/E
D
C♯m
Bm7
D6

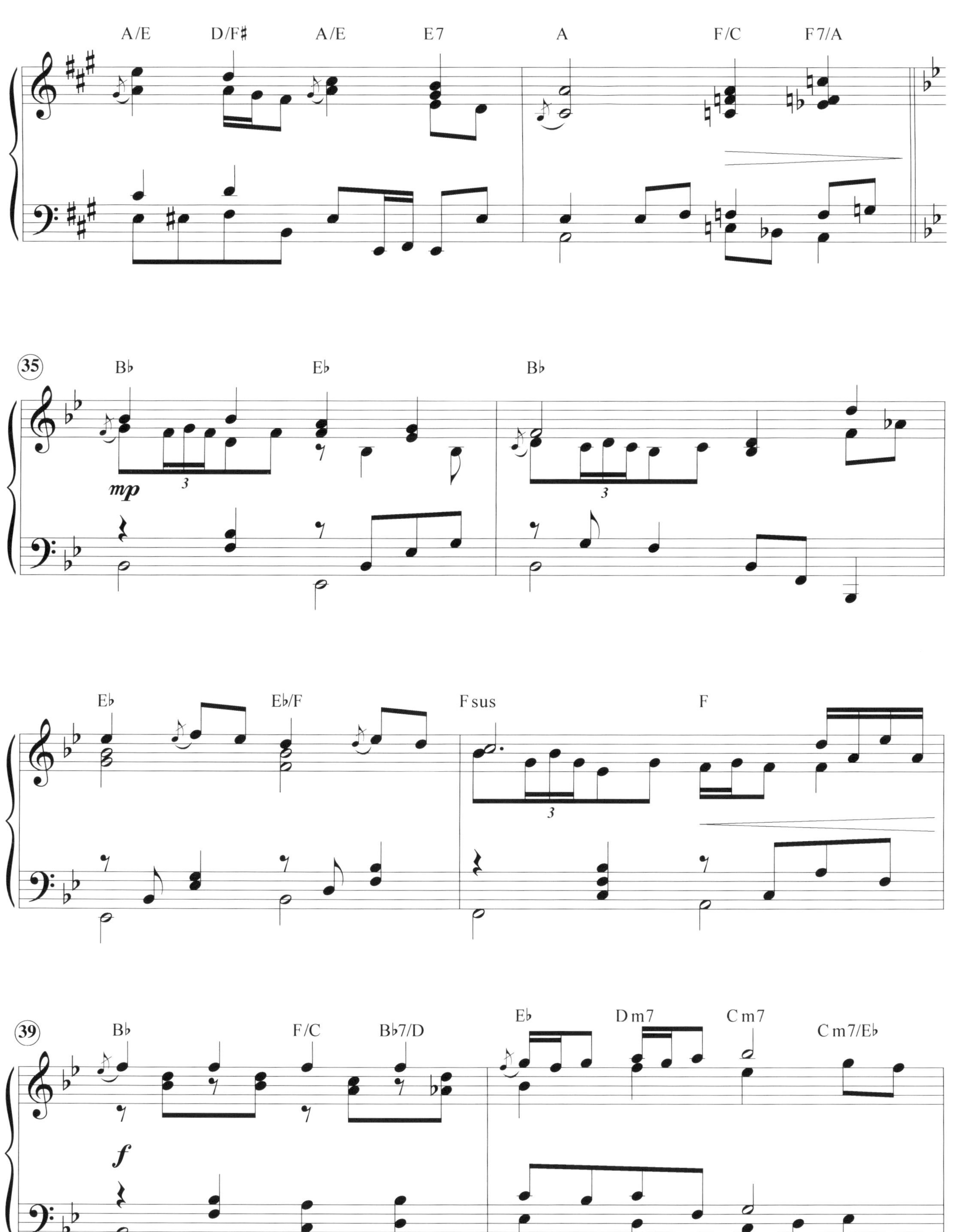
A/E
D/F♯
A/E
E7
A
F/C
F7/A
35
B♭
E♭
B♭
mp
3
3
E♭
E♭/F
F sus
F
3
39
B♭
F/C
B♭7/D
E♭
D m7
C m7
C m7/E♭
f

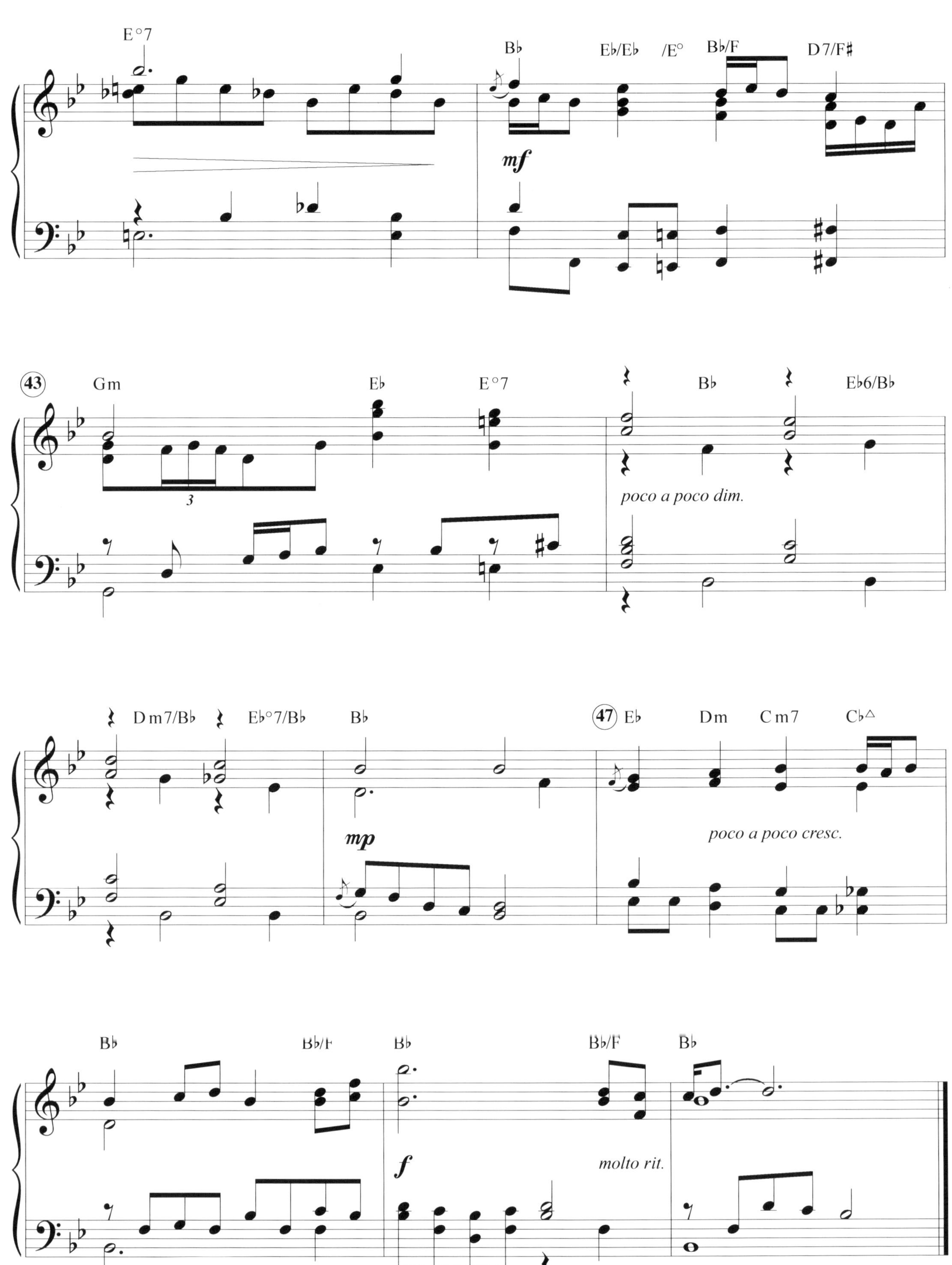
E°7
B♭
E♭/E♭
/E°
B♭/F
D7/F♯
mf
43
Gm
E♭
E°7
3
B♭
E♭6/B♭
poco a poco dim.
Dm7/B♭
E♭°7/B♭
B♭
mp
47
E♭
Dm
Cm7
C♭△
poco a poco cresc.
B♭
B♭/F
B♭
B♭/F
B♭
f
molto rit.

Brethren, We Have Met To Worship

George Atkins

William Moore
Arr. Darrell V. Archer

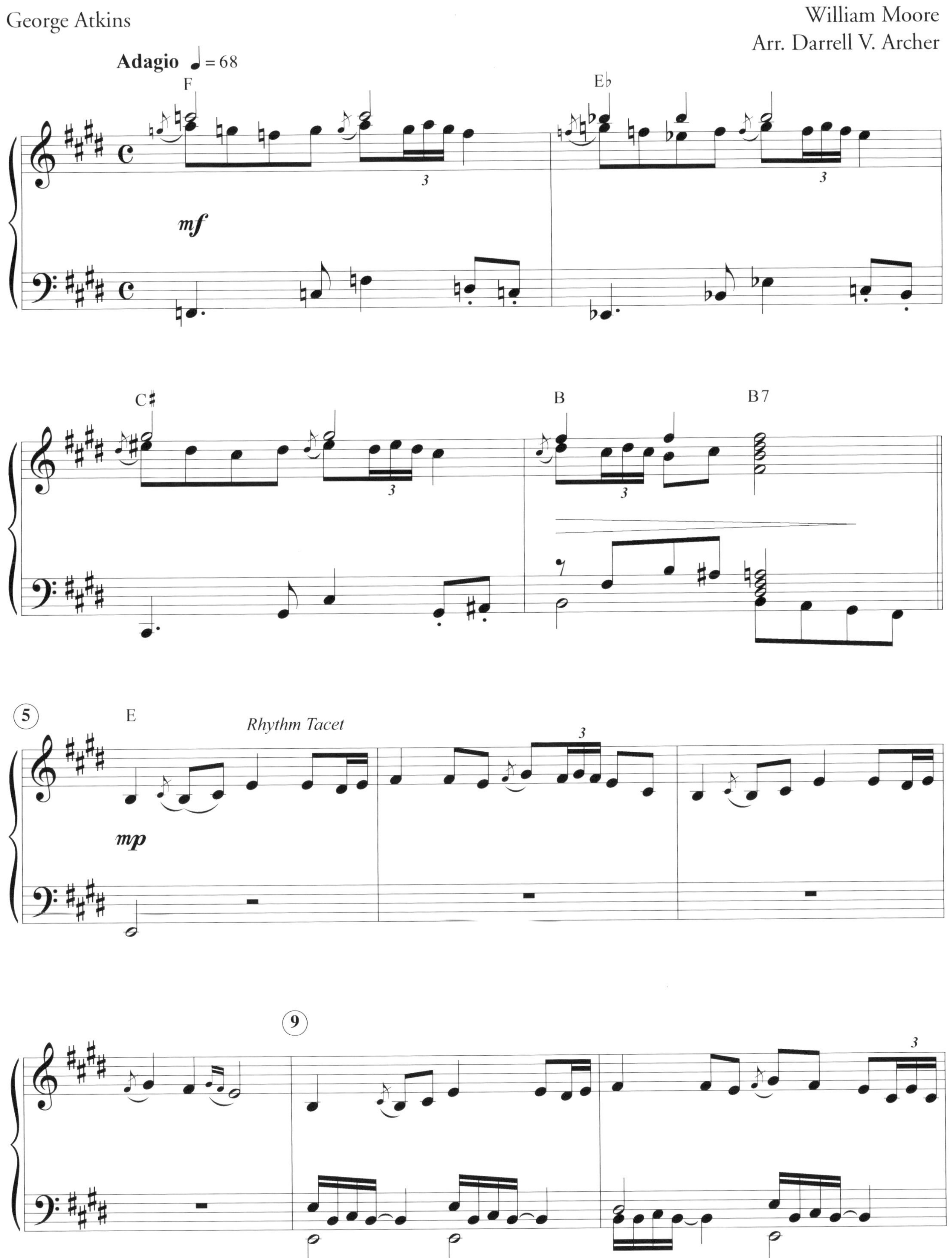

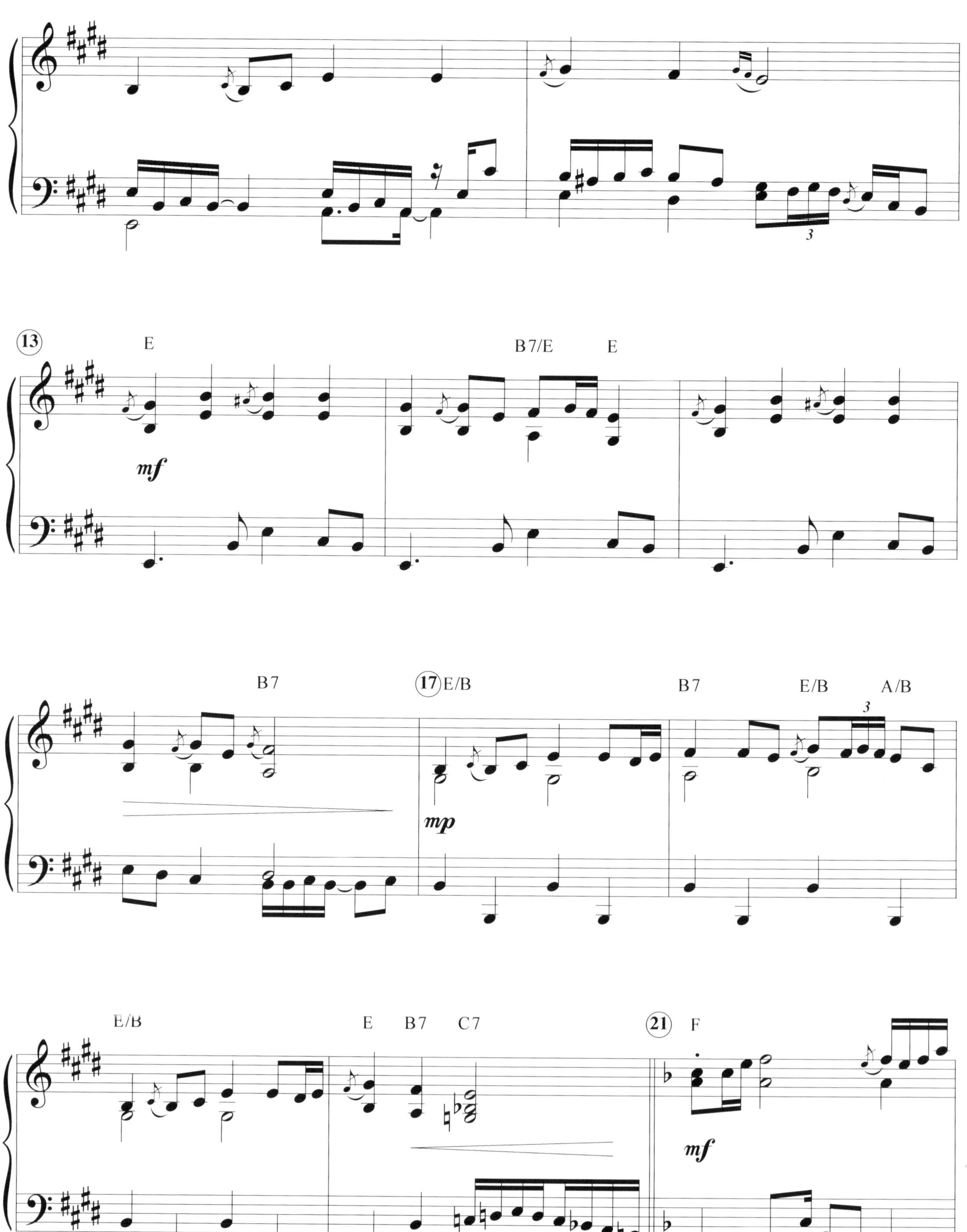

13
E
mf
B7/E
E
B7
17
E/B
mp
B7
E/B
A/B
3
3
E/B
E
B7
C7
21
F
mf

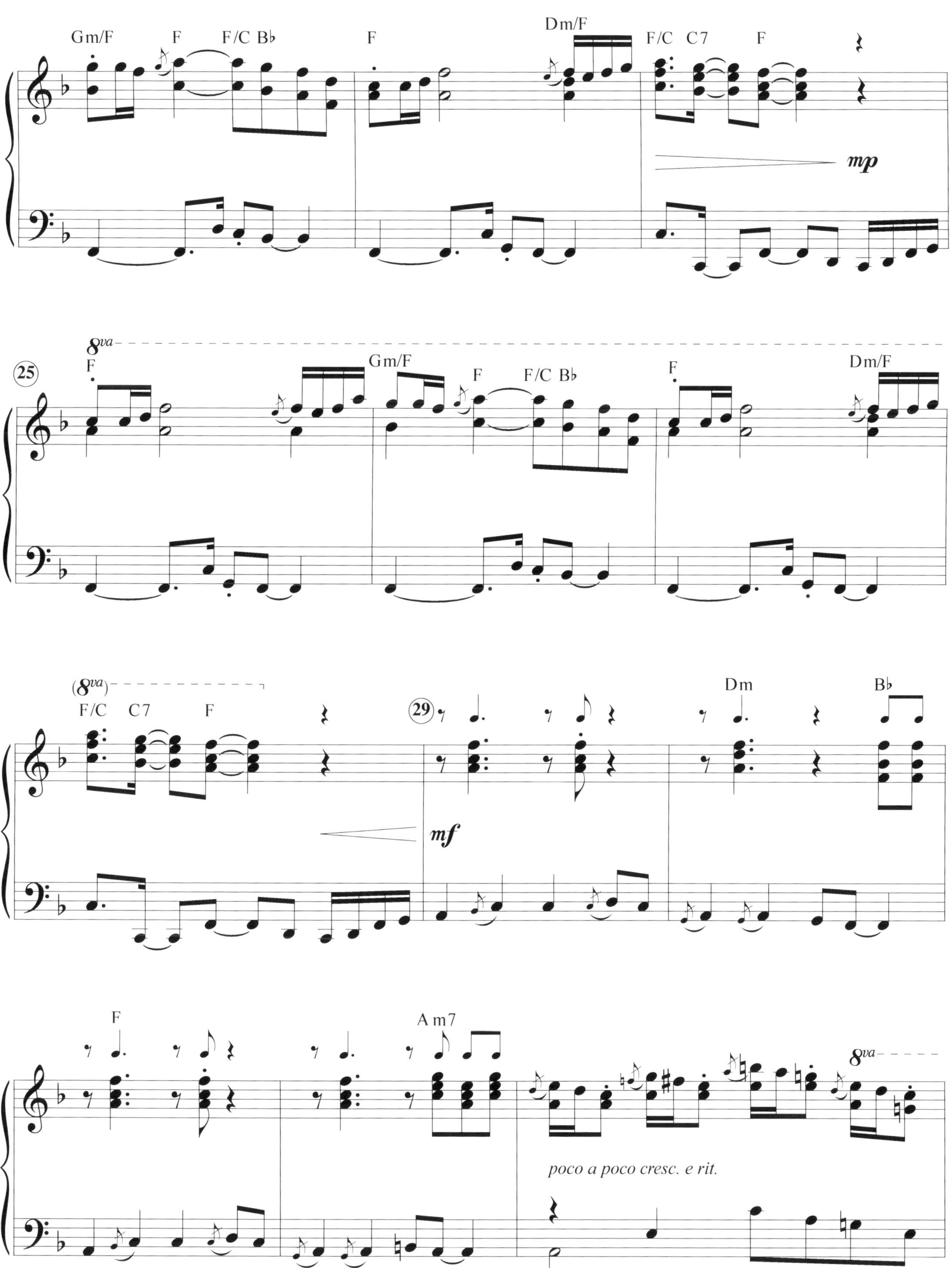
Gm/F
F
F/C
B♭
F
Dm/F
F/C
C7
F
mp
25
8va
F
Gm/F
F
F/C
B♭
F
Dm/F
(8va)
F/C
C7
F
29
Dm
B♭
mf
F
Am7
8va
poco a poco cresc. e rit.

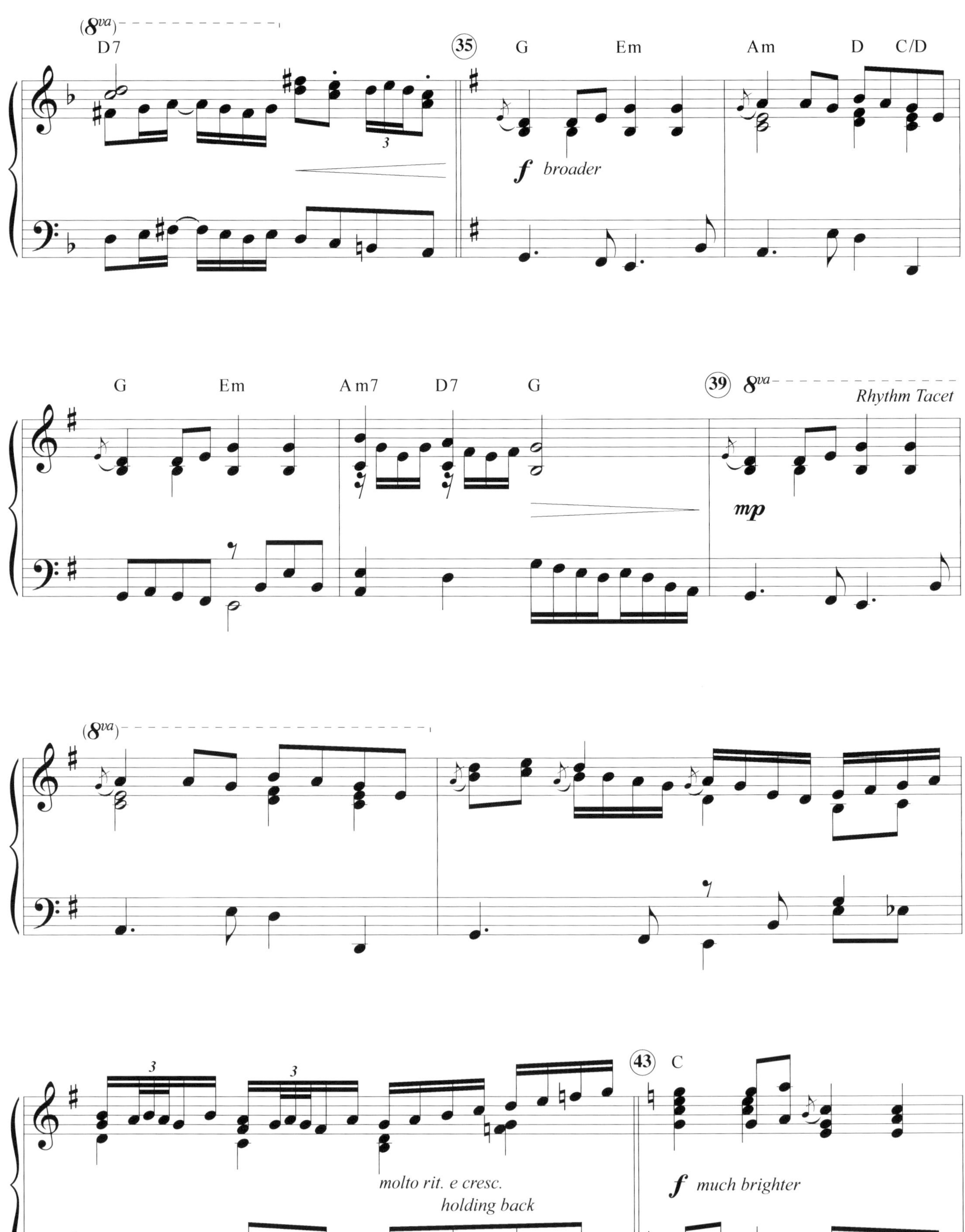
(8va)
D7
35
G
Em
Am
D
C/D
f broader
G
Em
Am7
D7
G
39
8va
Rhythm Tacet
mp
(8va)
43
C
molto rit. e cresc.
holding back
f much brighter

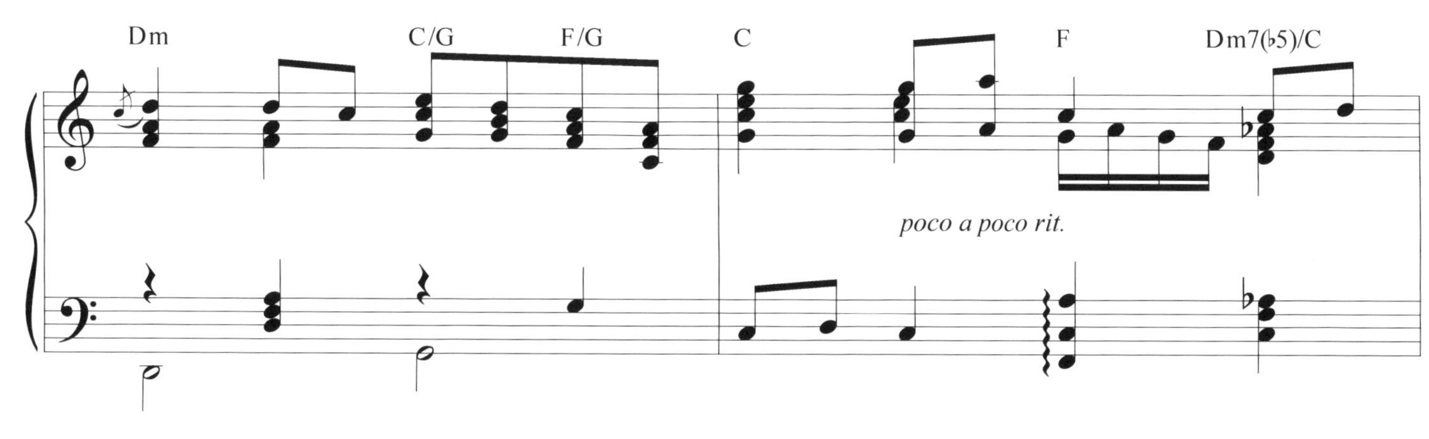

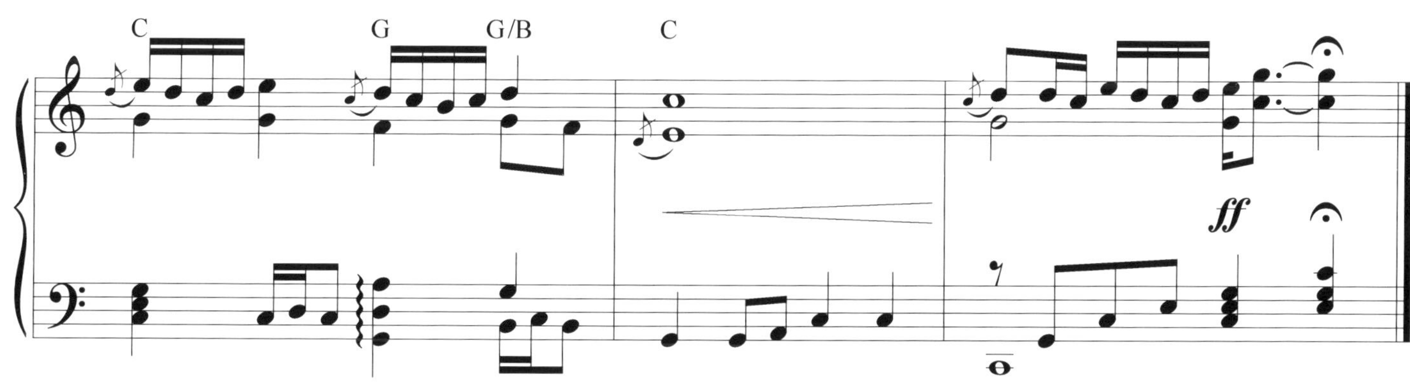

Rejoice always;
pray without ceasing;
in everything give thanks;
for this is God's will
for you in Christ Jesus.

1 Thessalonians 5:16-18 (LSB)

Come, Ye Thankful People, Come

George J. Elvey
Arr. Darrell V. Archer

Henry Alford

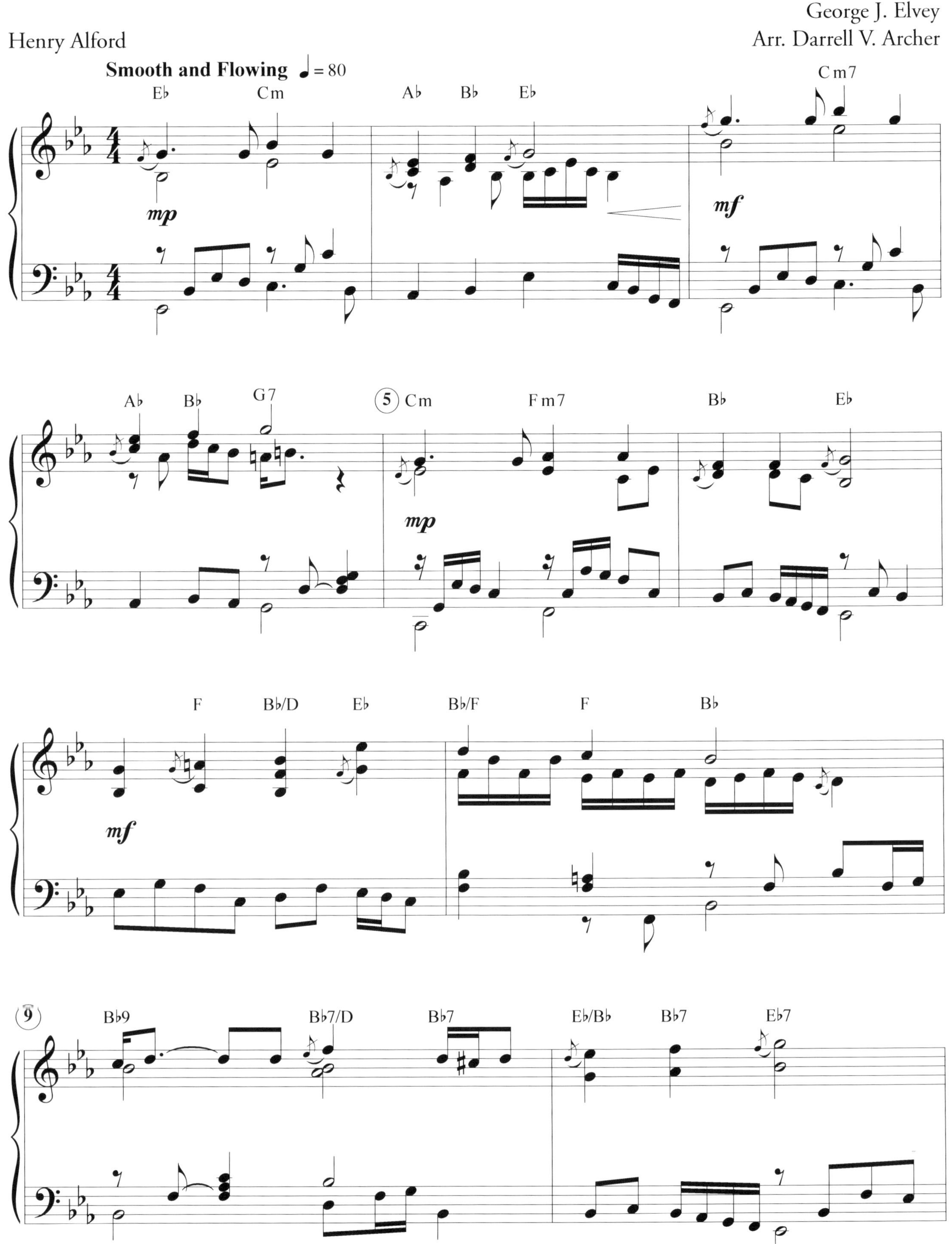

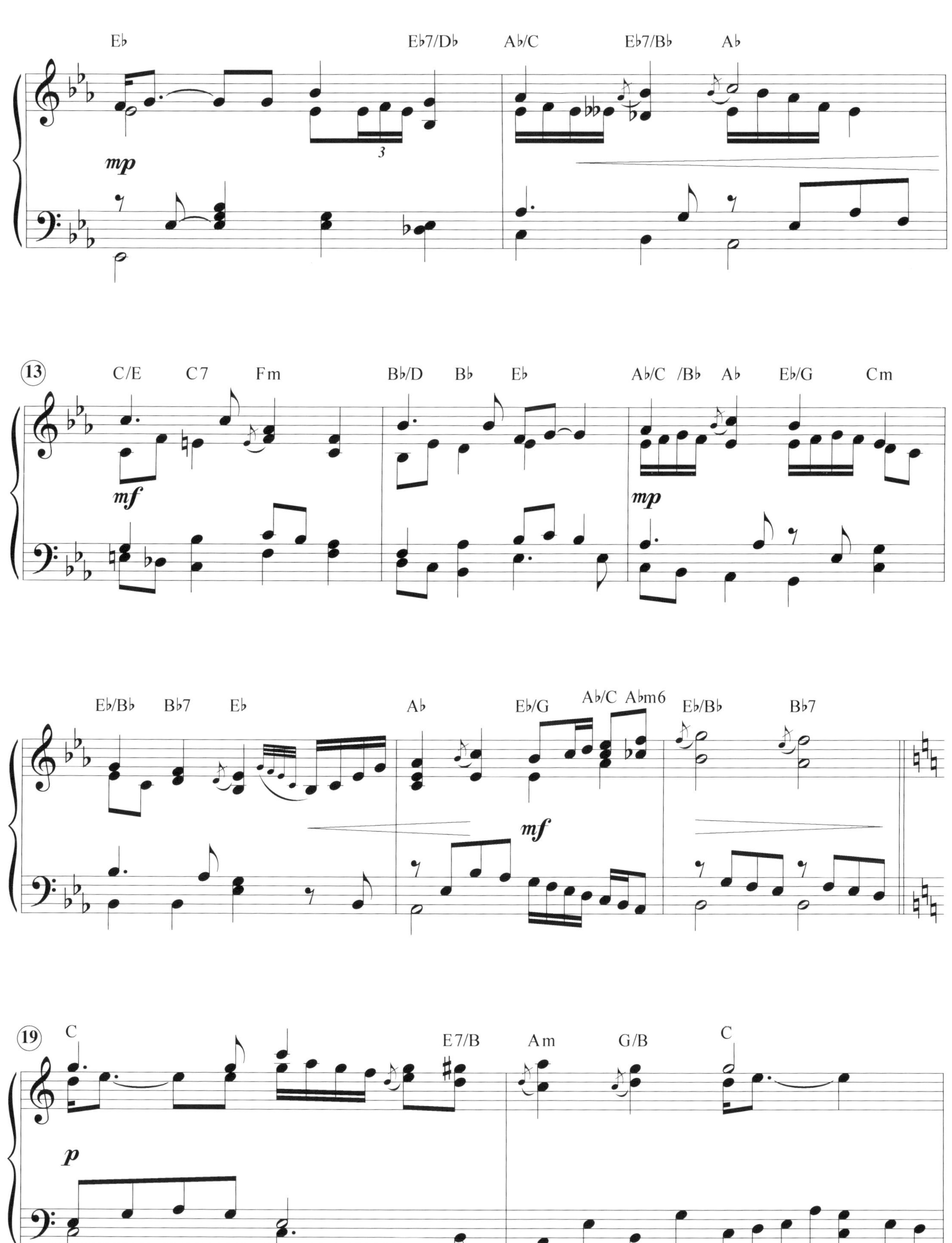
E♭
E♭7/D♭
A♭/C
E♭7/B♭
A♭
mp
3
13
C/E
C7
Fm
B♭/D
B♭
E♭
A♭/C
/B♭
A♭
E♭/G
Cm
mf
mp
E♭/B♭
B♭7
E♭
A♭
E♭/G
A♭/C
A♭m6
E♭/B♭
B♭7
mf
19
C
E7/B
Am
G/B
C
p

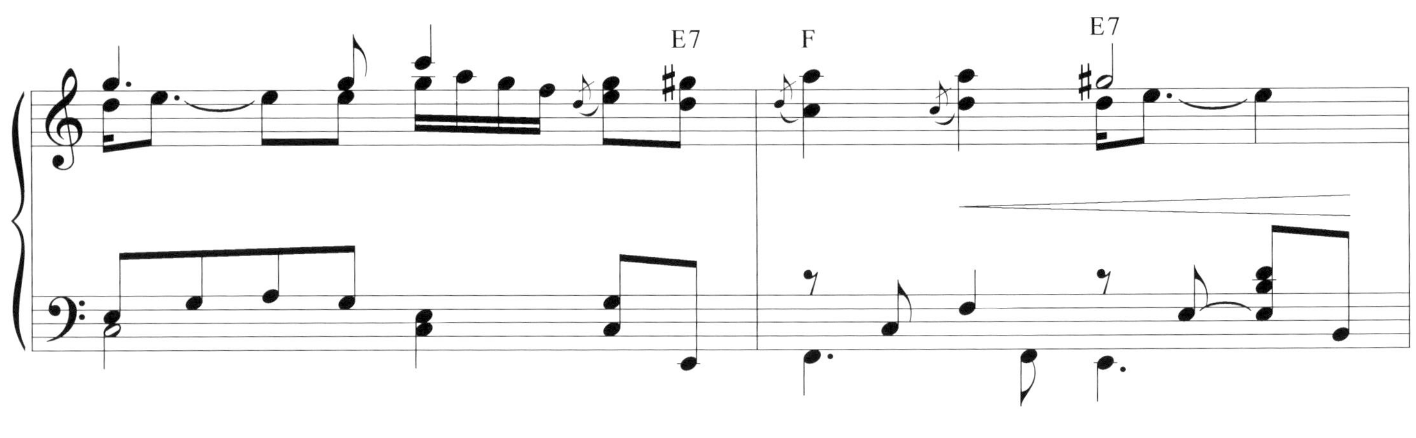
E7
F
E7

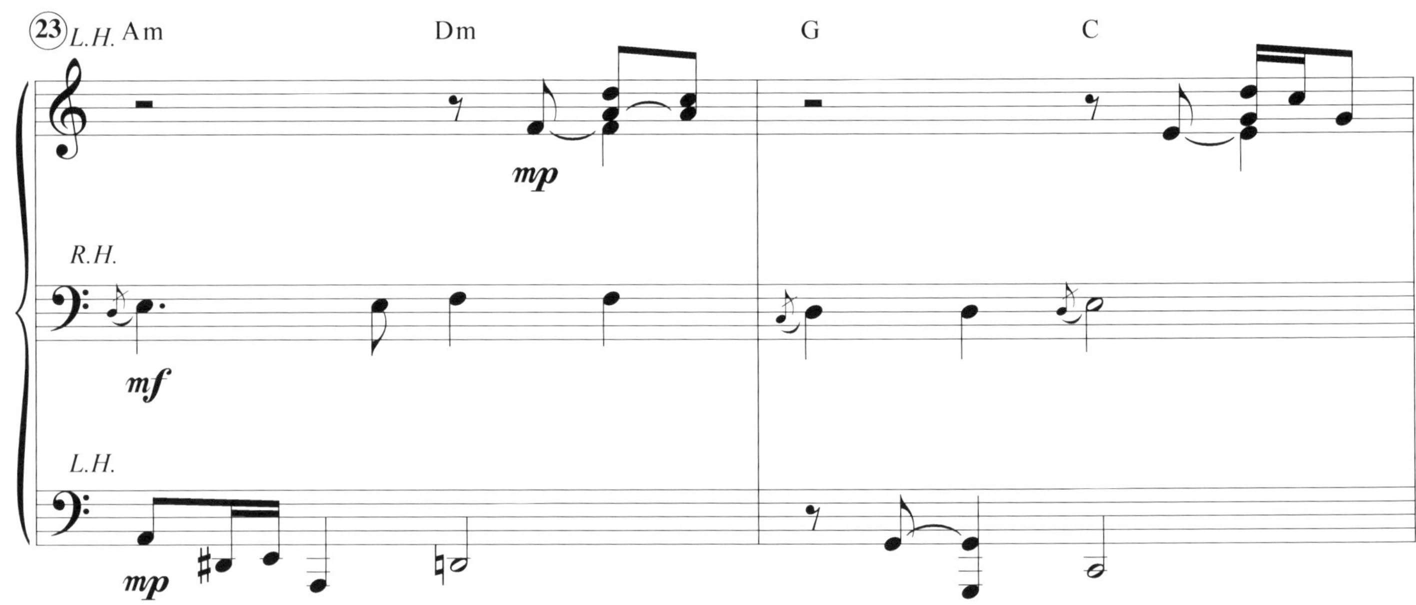
23
L.H.
Am
Dm
G
C
mp
R.H.
mf
L.H.
mp

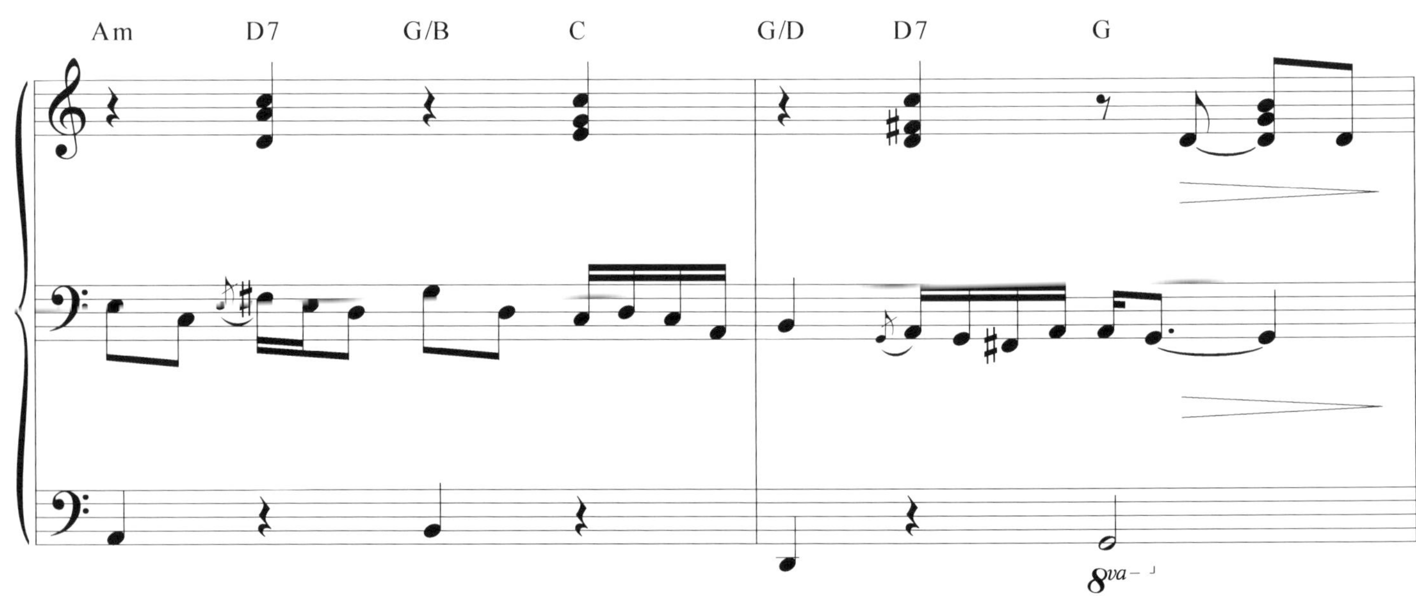
Am
D7
G/B
C
G/D
D7
G
8va

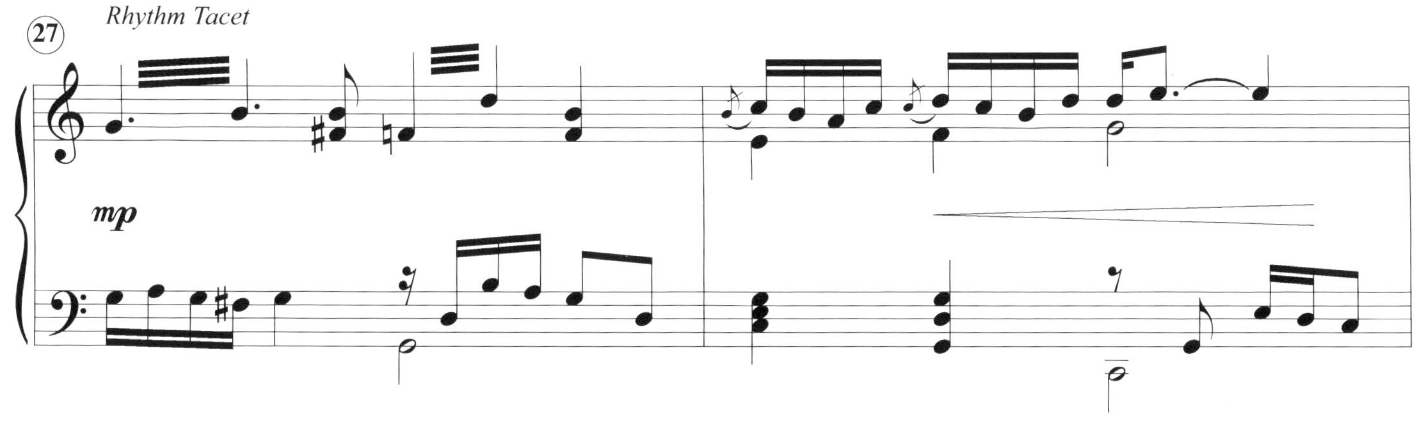
27
Rhythm Tacet
mp

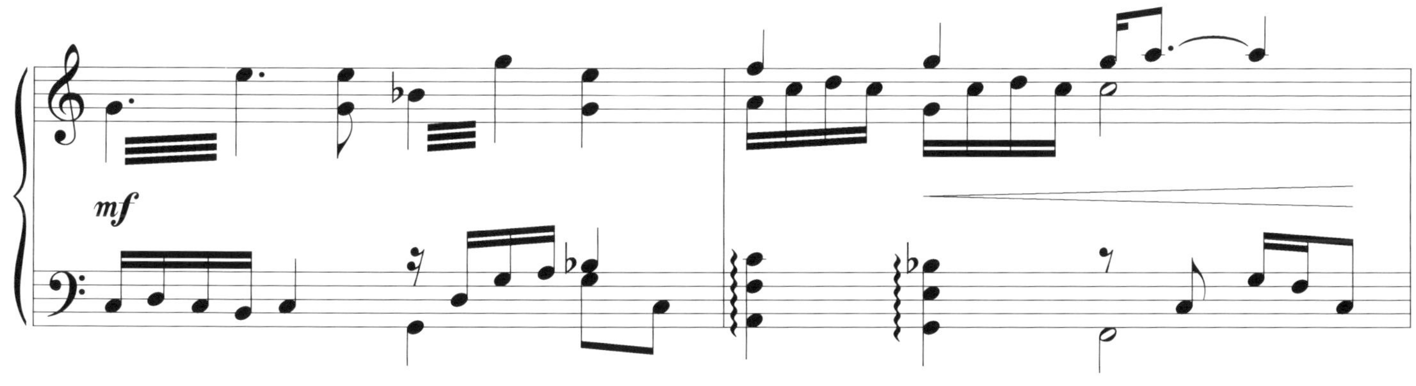
mf

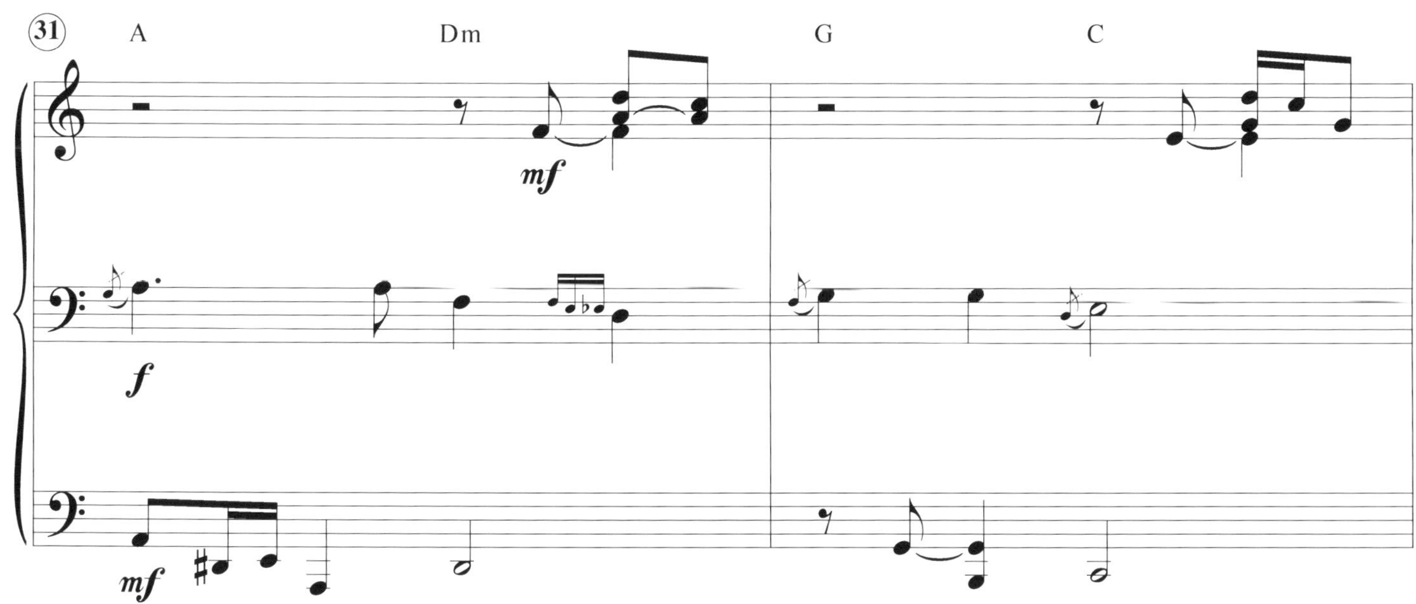
31
A
Dm
G
C
mf
f
mf

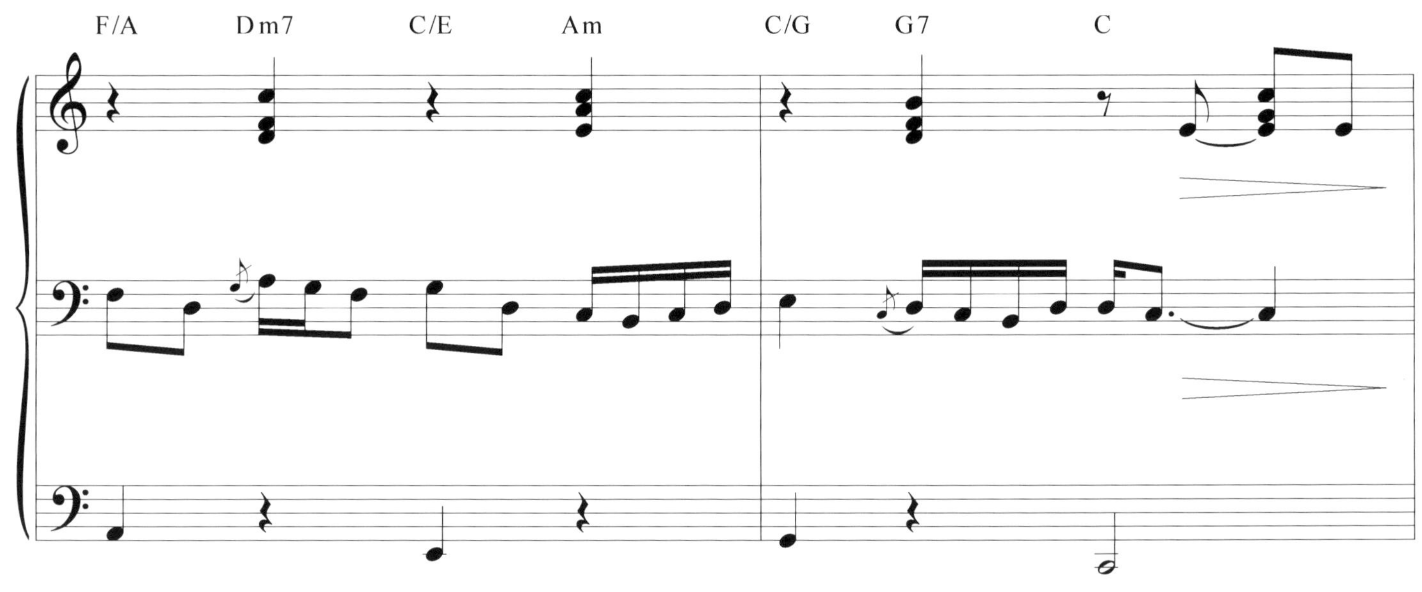
F/A
Dm7
C/E
Am
C/G
G7
C

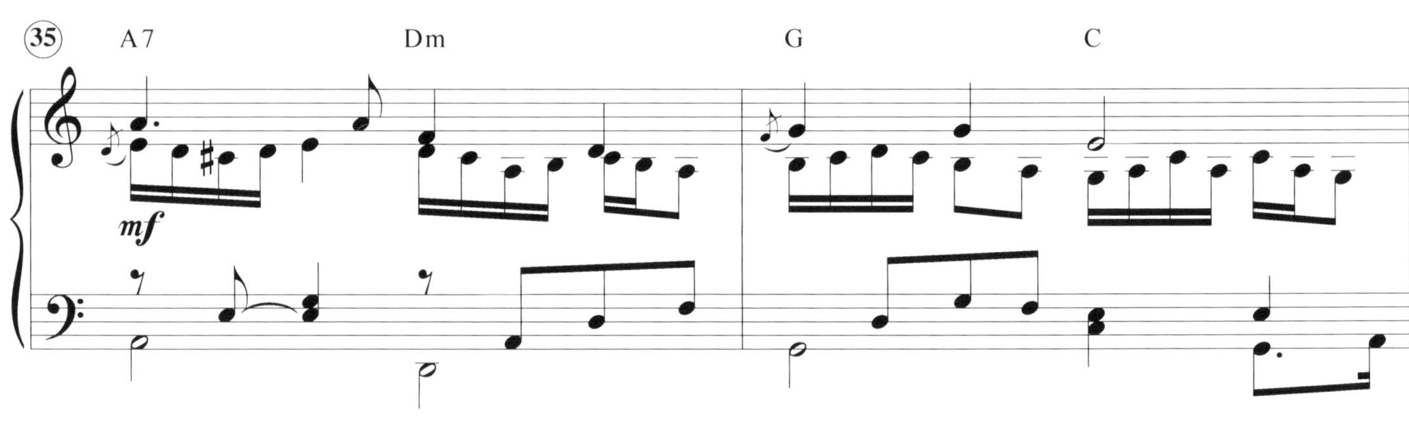
35
A7
Dm
G
C
mf

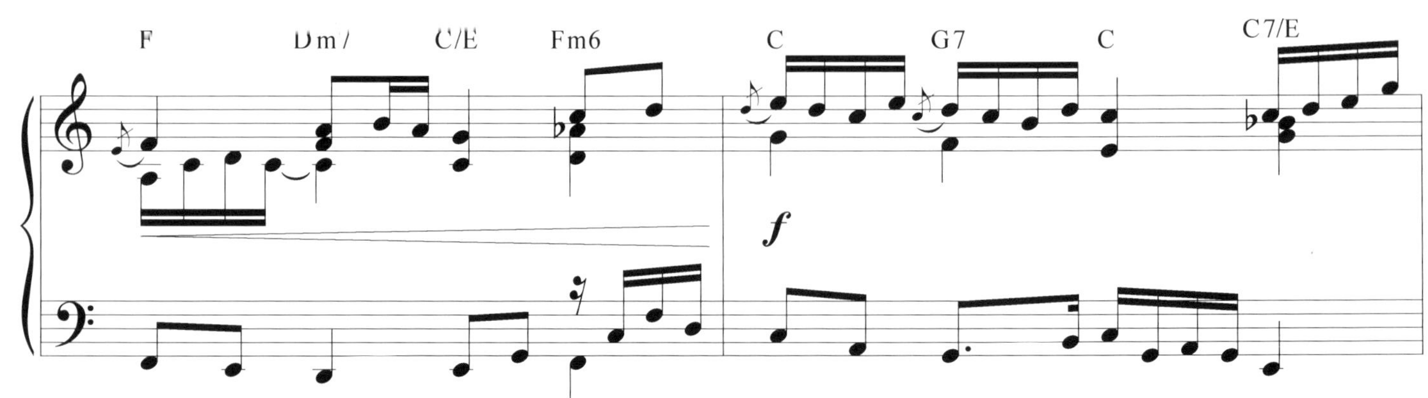
F
Dm7
C/E
Fm6
C
G7
C
C7/E
f

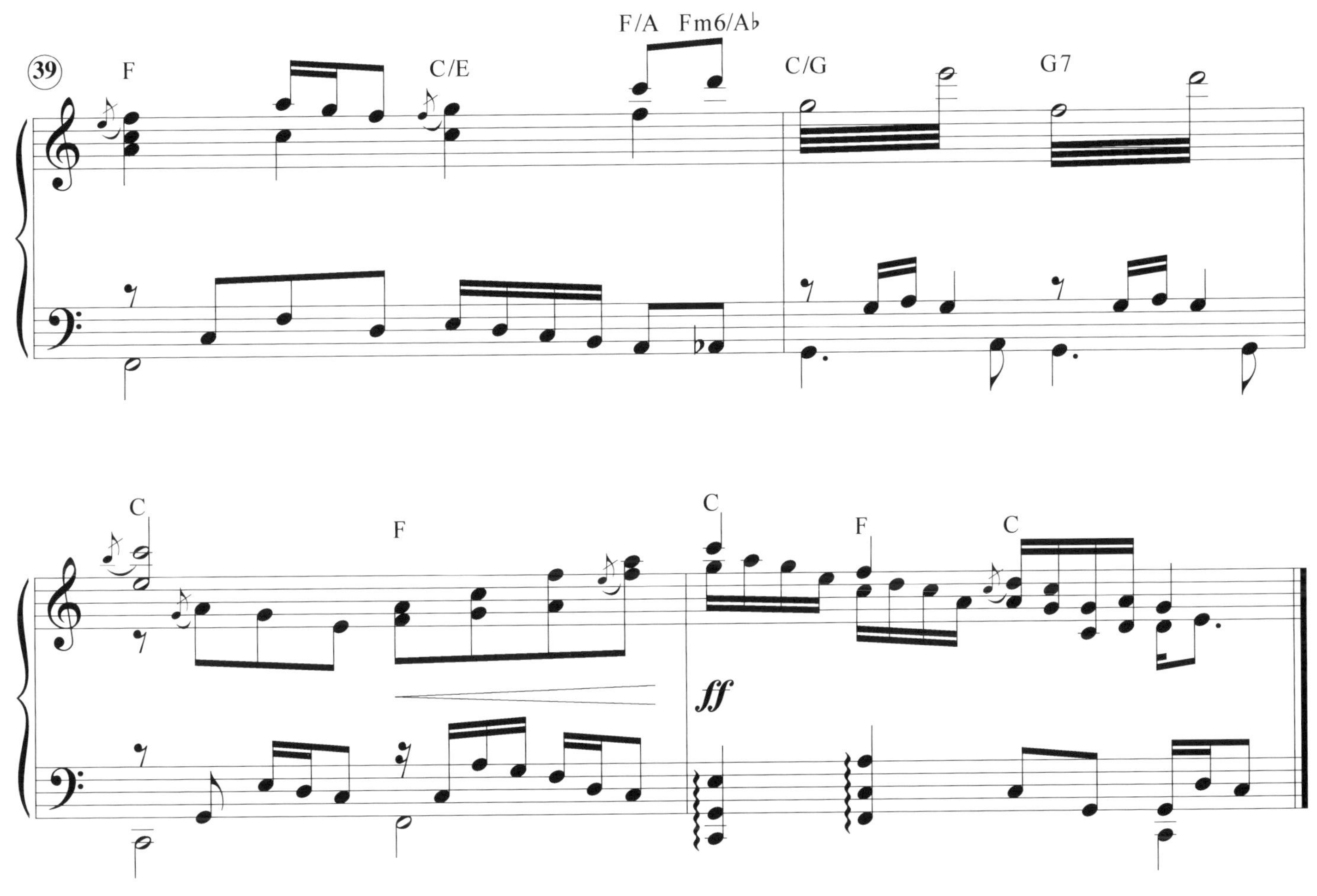

Oh give thanks to the LORD, for He is good; for His steadfast love endures forever!

1 Chronicles 16:34 (ESV)

Count Your Blessings

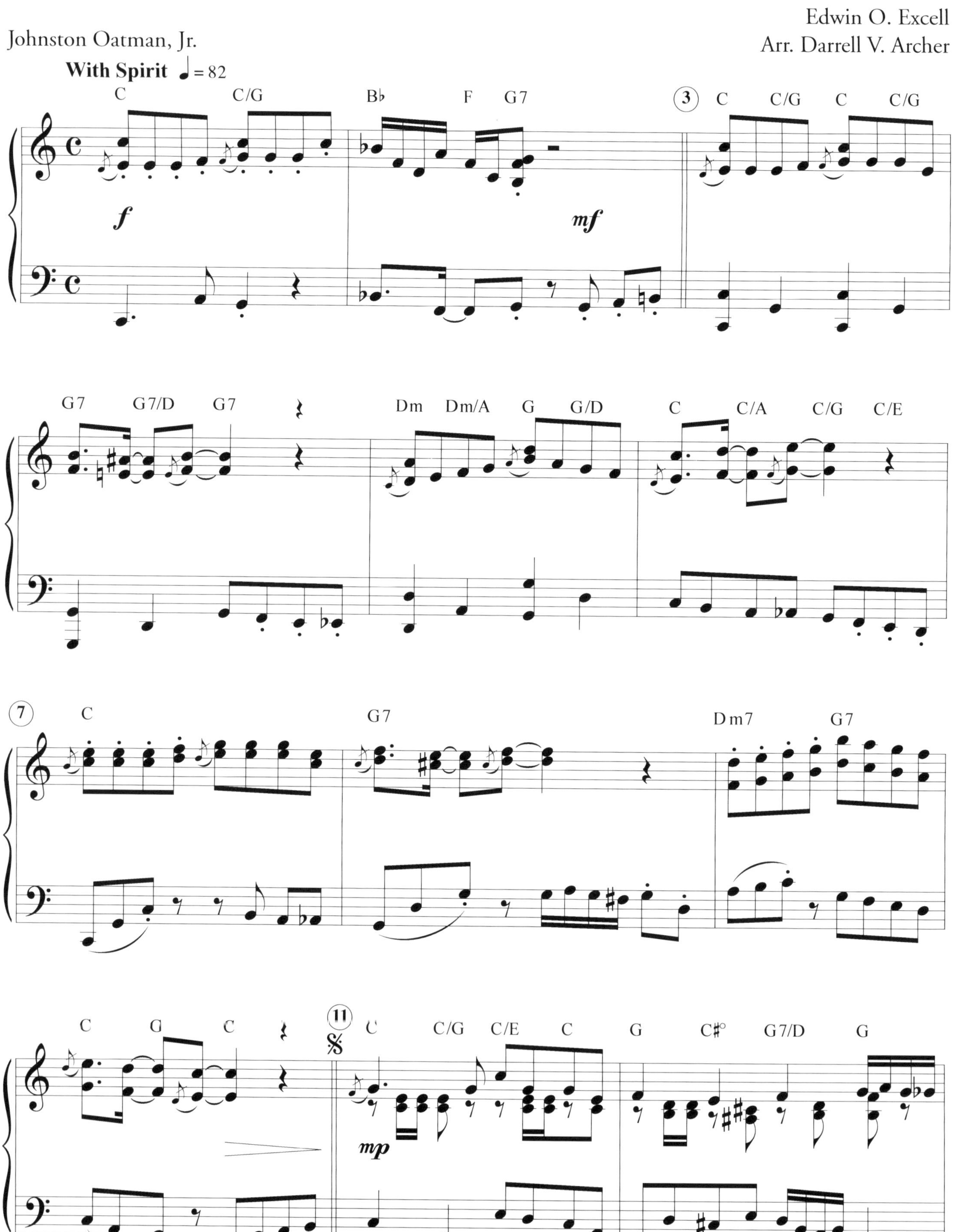

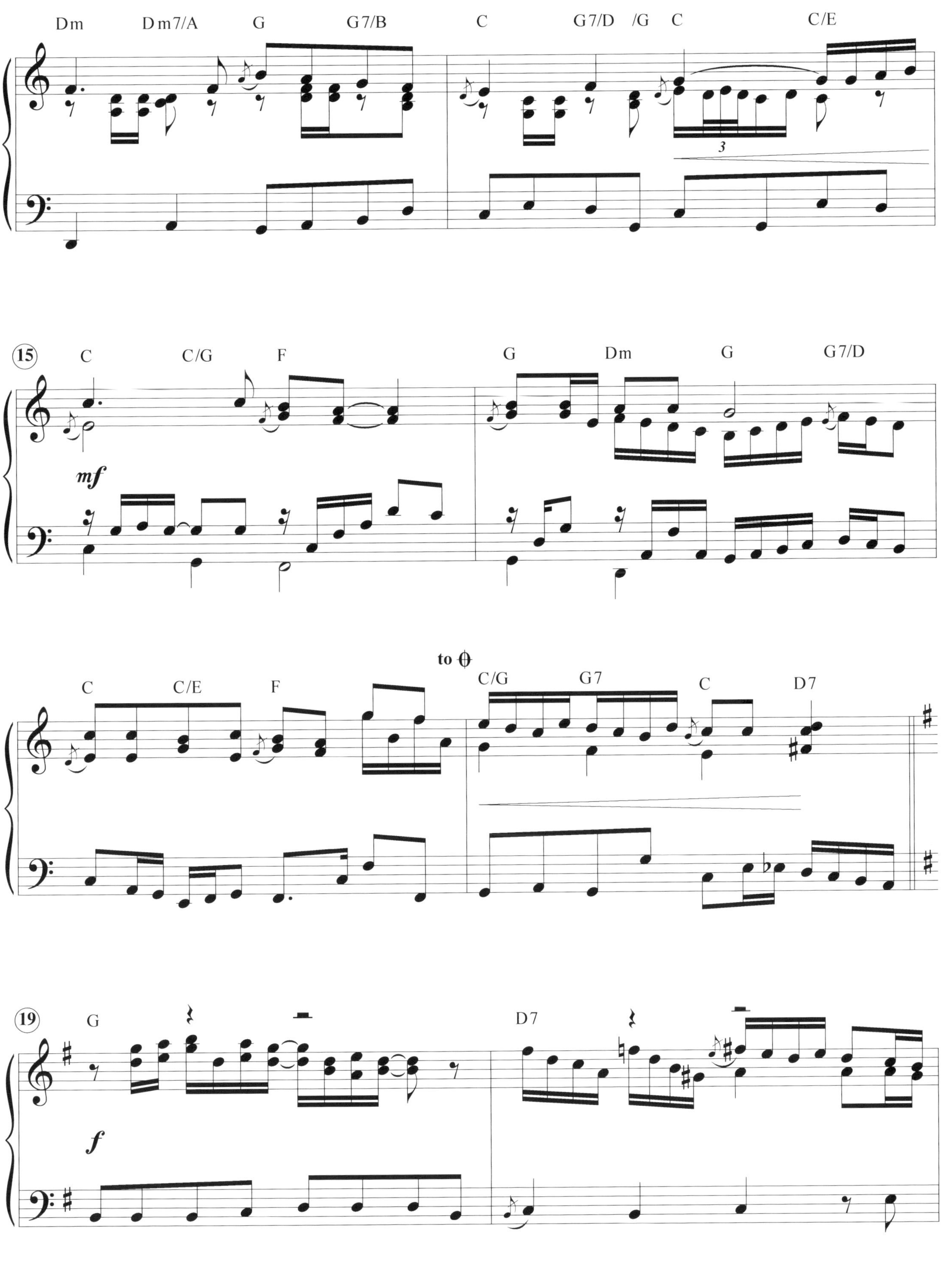

Dm Dm7/A G G7/B C G7/D /G C C/E

3

15 C C/G F G Dm G G7/D

mf

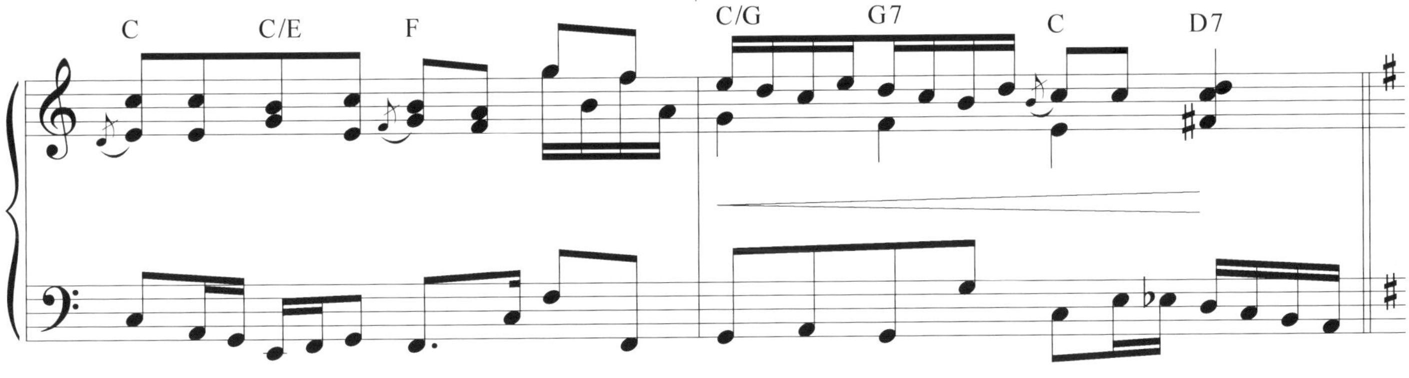

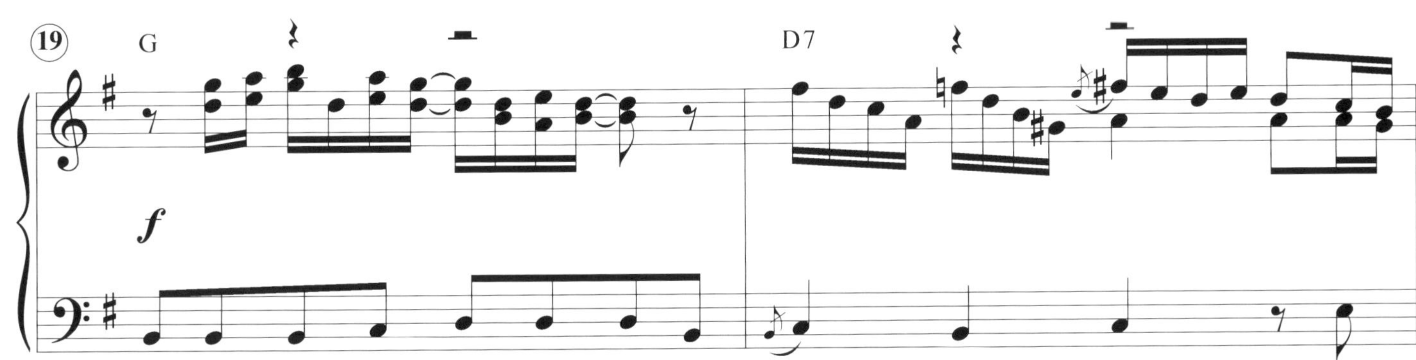

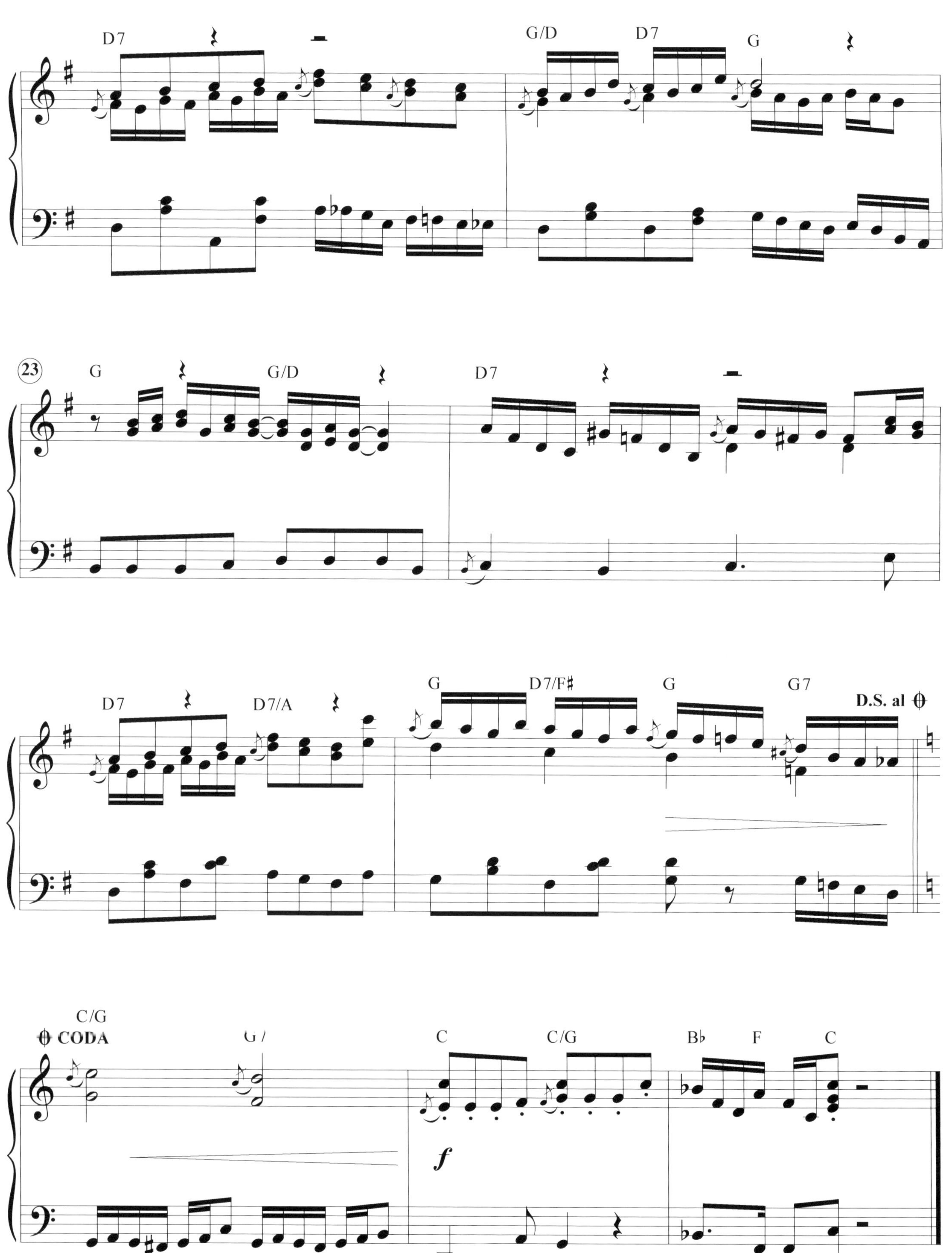
D7
G/D
D7
G
23
G
G/D
D7
D7
D7/A
G
D7/F♯
G
G7
D.S. al ⊕
C/G
⊕ CODA
C
C/G
B♭
F
C
f

Let The Whole Creation Cry

Robert Williams
Arr. Darrell V. Archer
Stopford A. Brooke

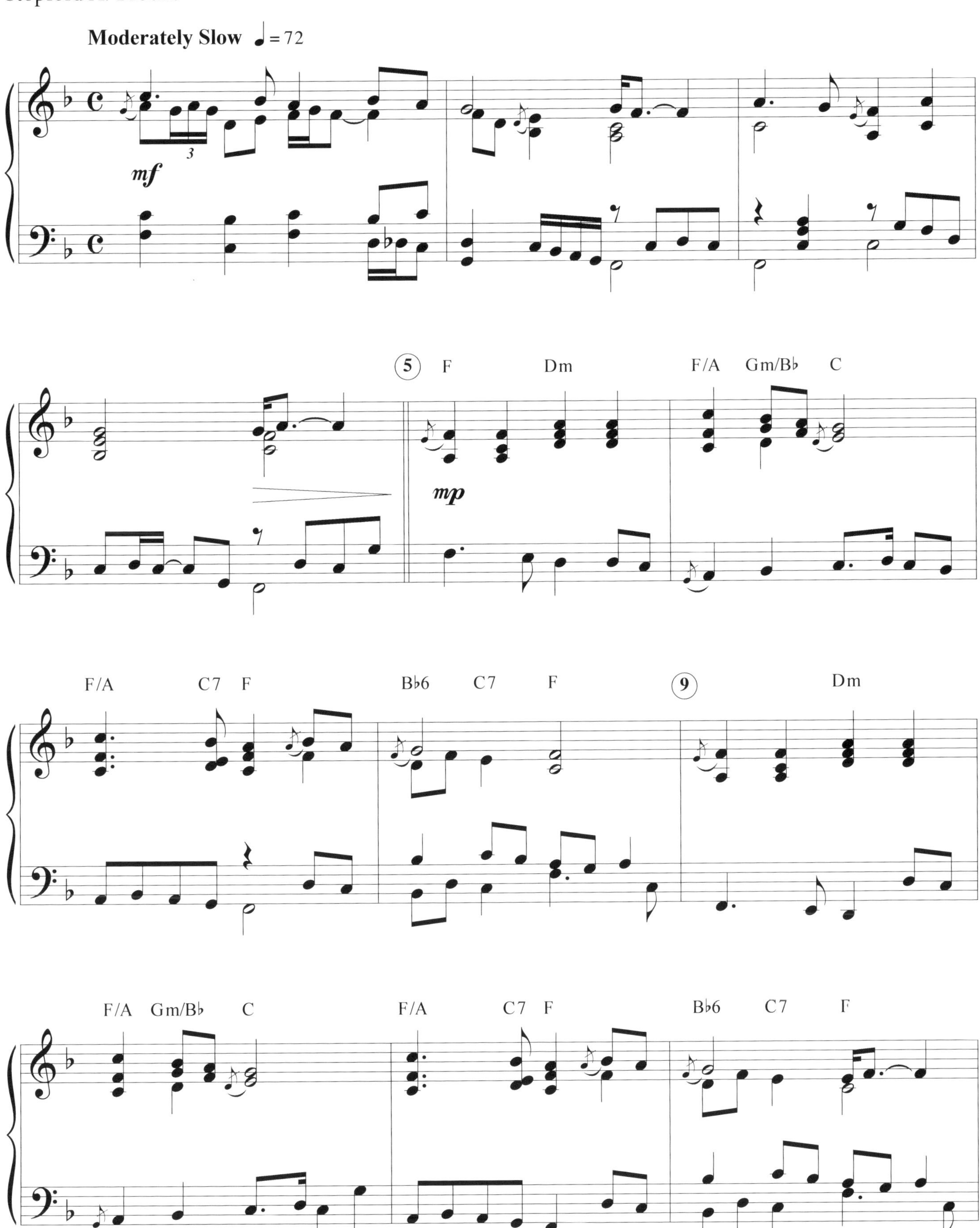

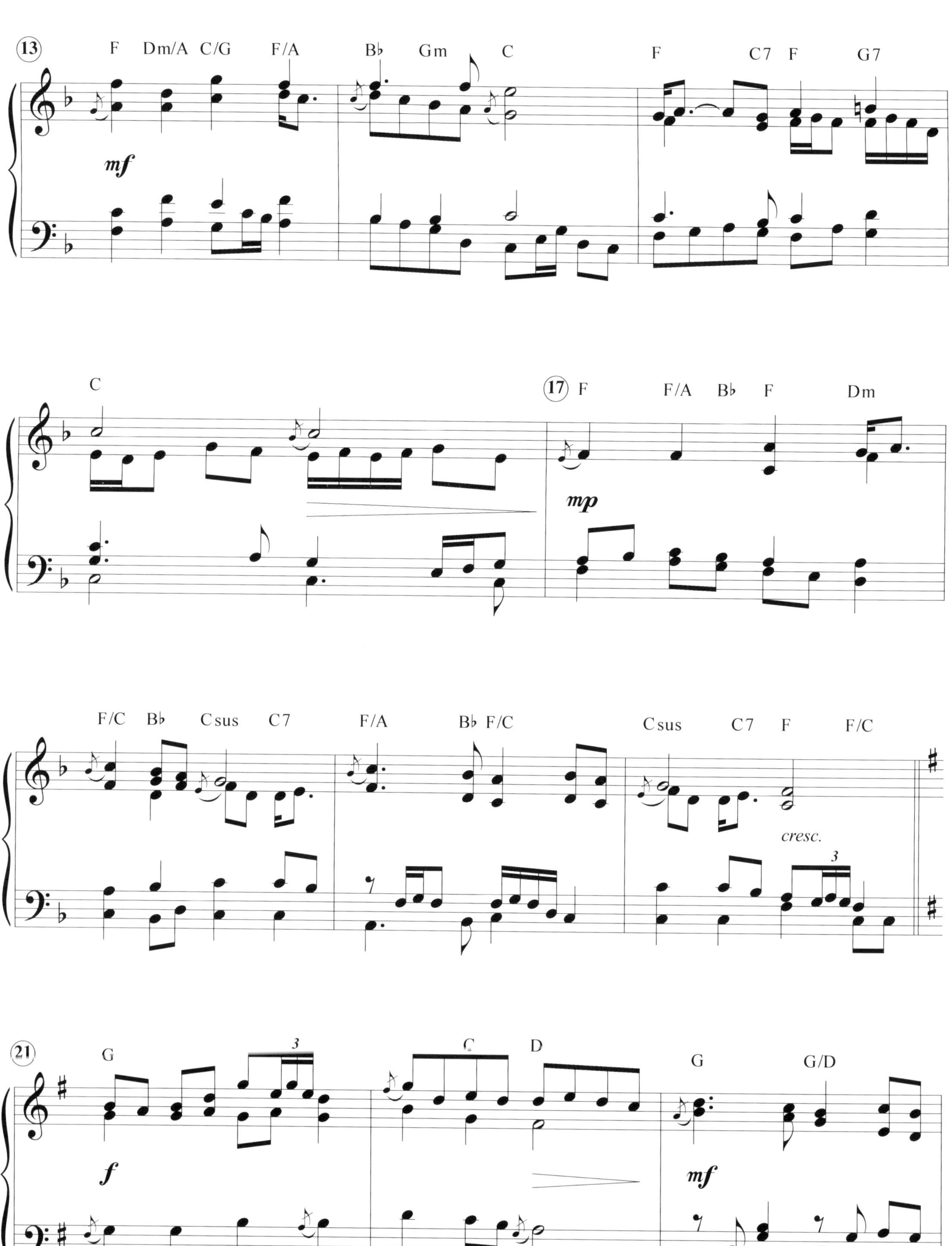
13
F
Dm/A
C/G
F/A
B♭
Gm
C
F
C7
F
G7
mf
C
17
F
F/A
B♭
F
Dm
mp
F/C
B♭
Csus
C7
F/A
B♭
F/C
Csus
C7
F
F/C
cresc.
3
21
G
3
C
D
G
G/D
f
mf

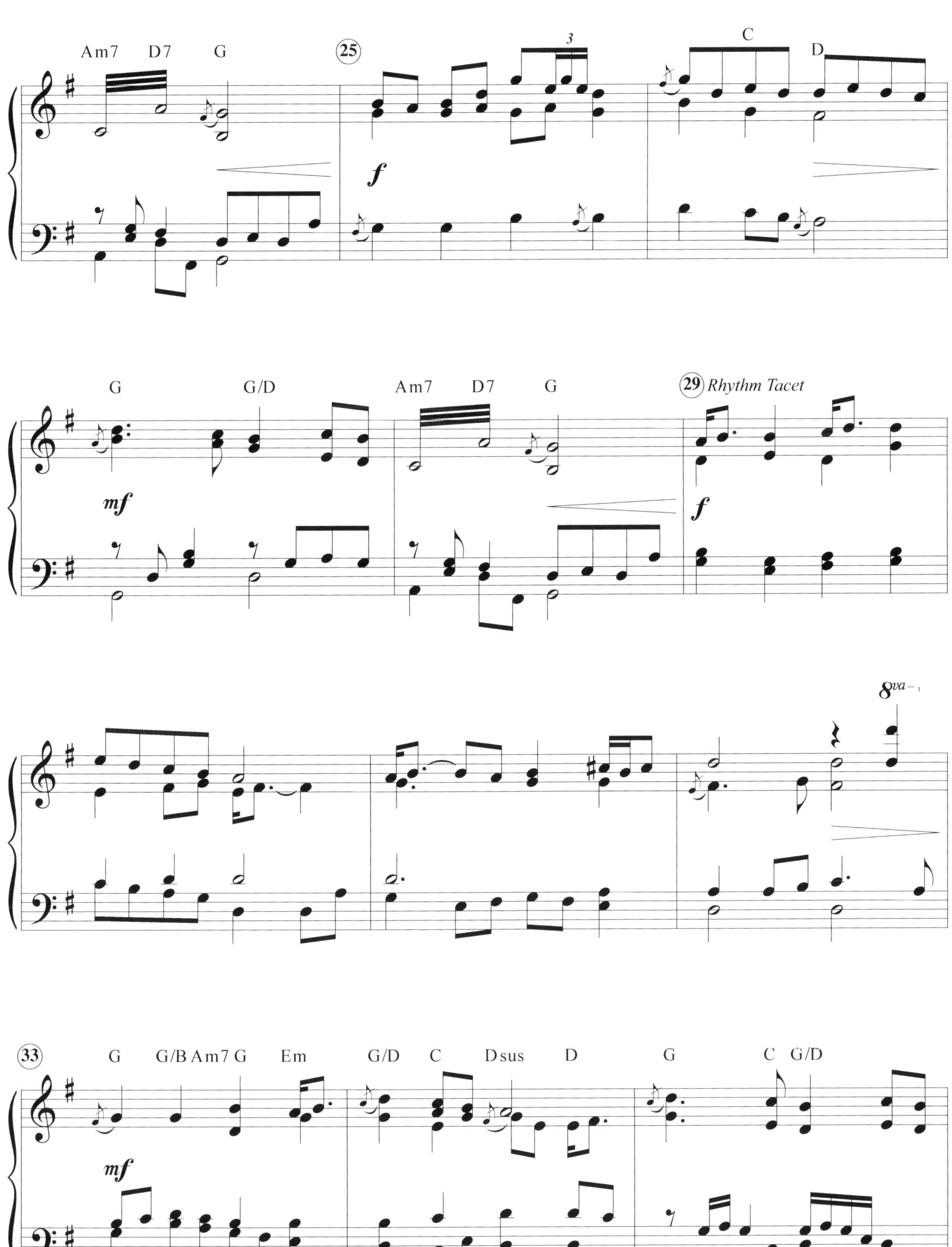
Am7 D7 G
25
3
f
C
D
G G/D
mf
Am7 D7 G
29 Rhythm Tacet
f
8va
33
G G/B Am7 G Em
mf
G/D C Dsus D
G C G/D

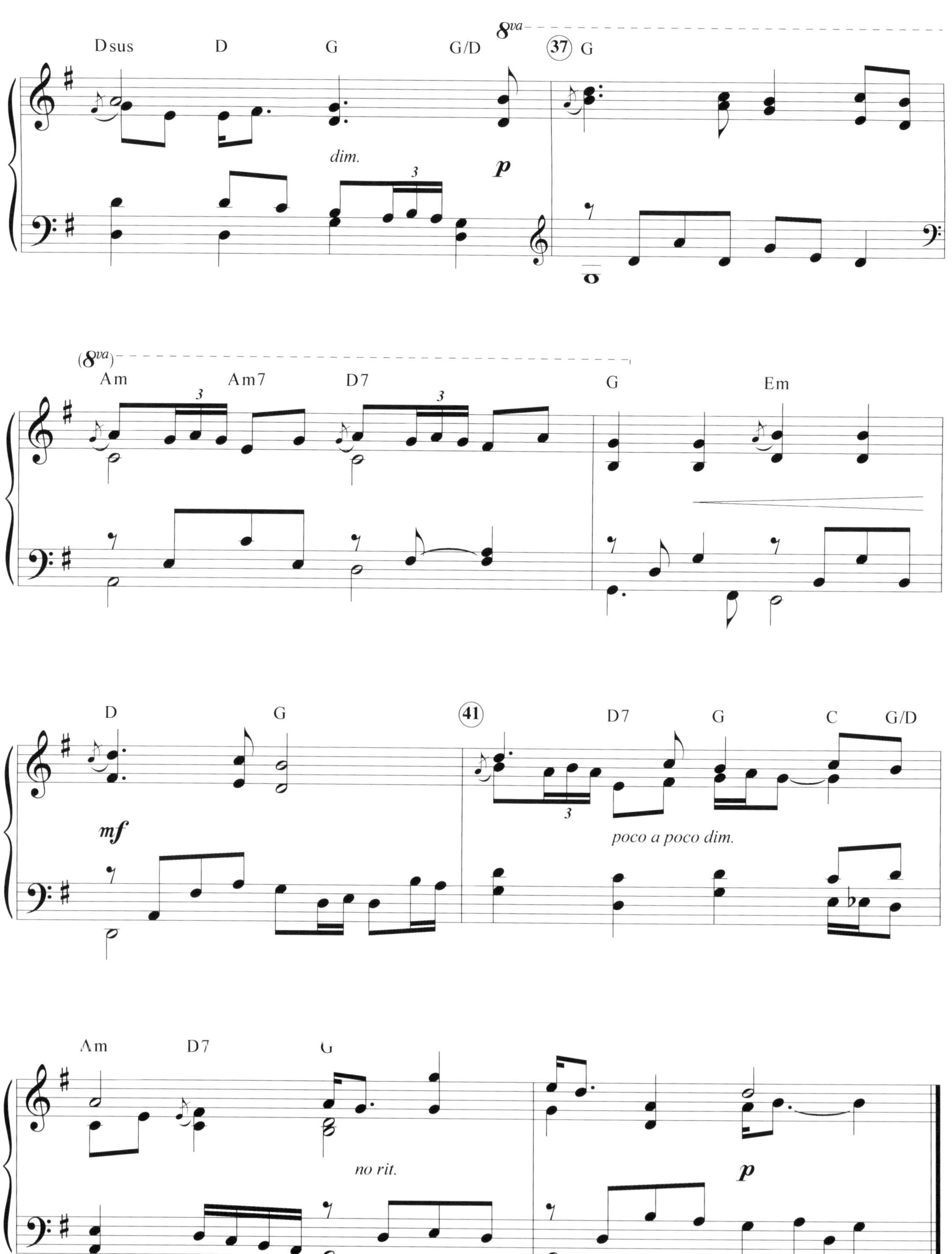
8va
Dsus
D
G
G/D
37
G
dim.
p
3
(8va)
Am
Am7
D7
G
Em
D
G
41
D7
G
C
G/D
mf
poco a poco dim.
Am
D7
G
no rit.
p

Now Thank We All Our God

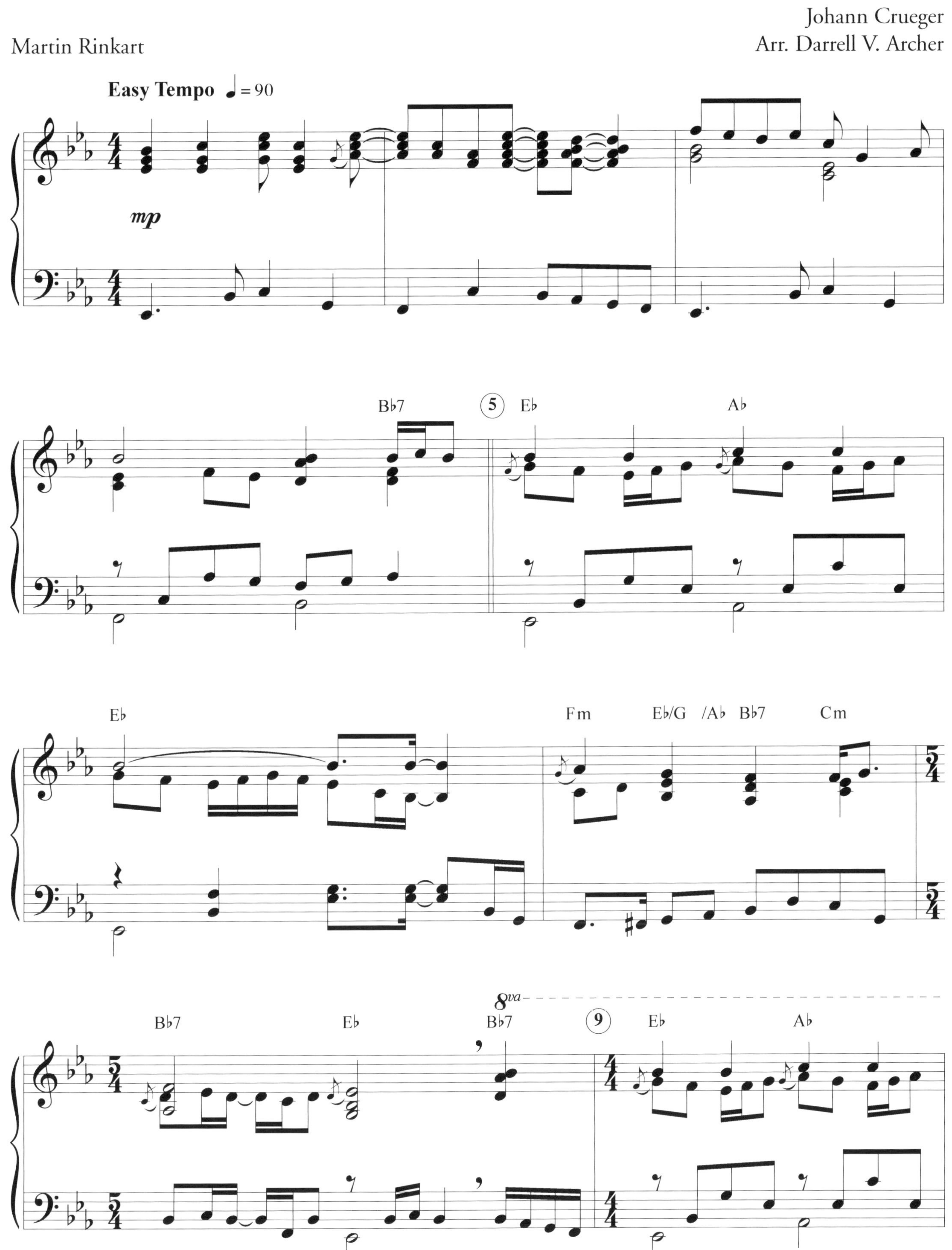

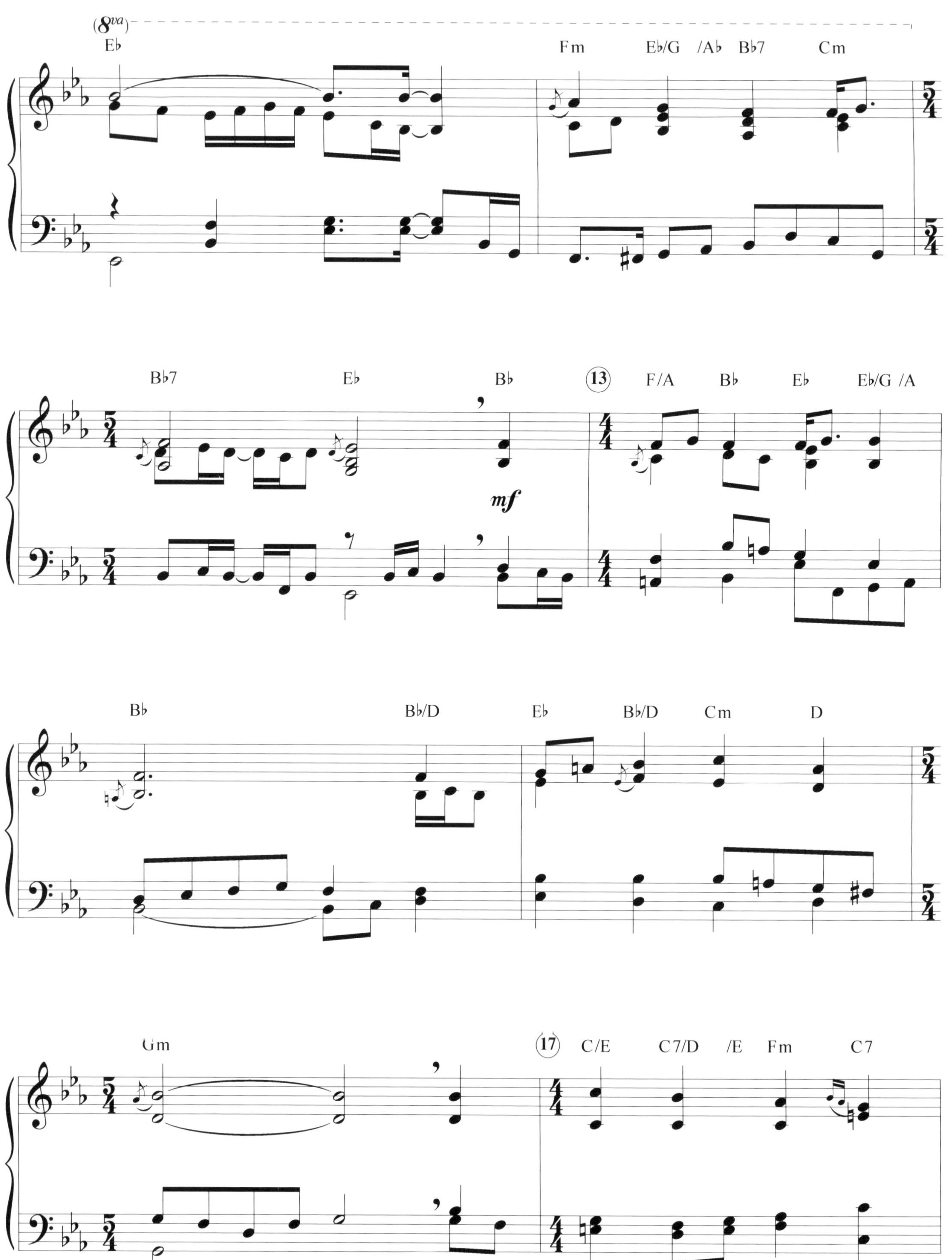
(8va)
E♭
Fm
E♭/G
/A♭
B♭7
Cm
B♭7
E♭
B♭
mf
13
F/A
B♭
E♭
E♭/G
/A
B♭
B♭/D
E♭
B♭/D
Cm
D
Gm
17
C/E
C7/D
/E
Fm
C7

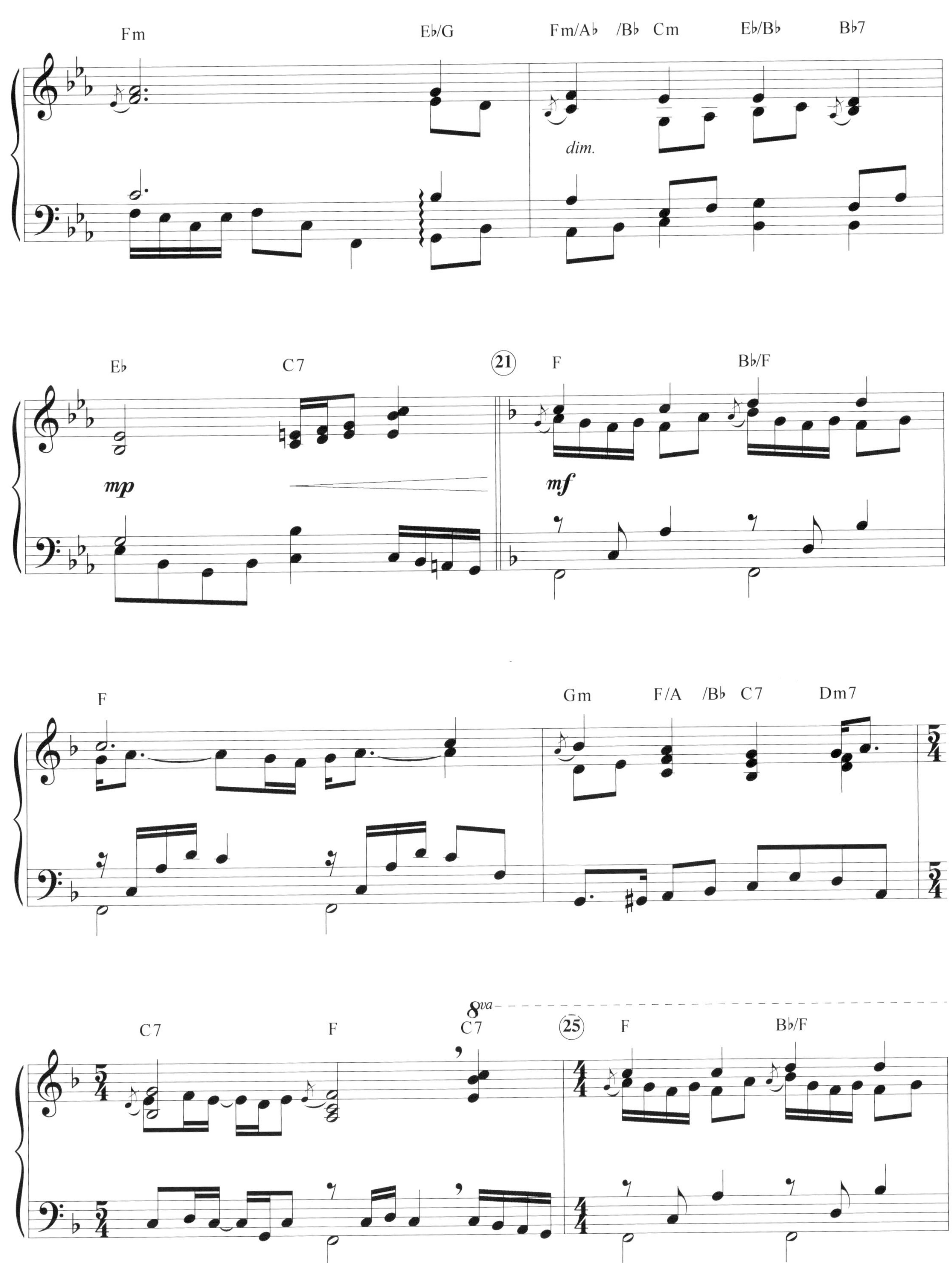
Fm
Eb/G
Fm/Ab
/Bb
Cm
Eb/Bb
Bb7
dim.
Eb
C7
21
F
Bb/F
mp
mf
F
Gm
F/A
/Bb
C7
Dm7
C7
F
C7
8va
25
F
Bb/F

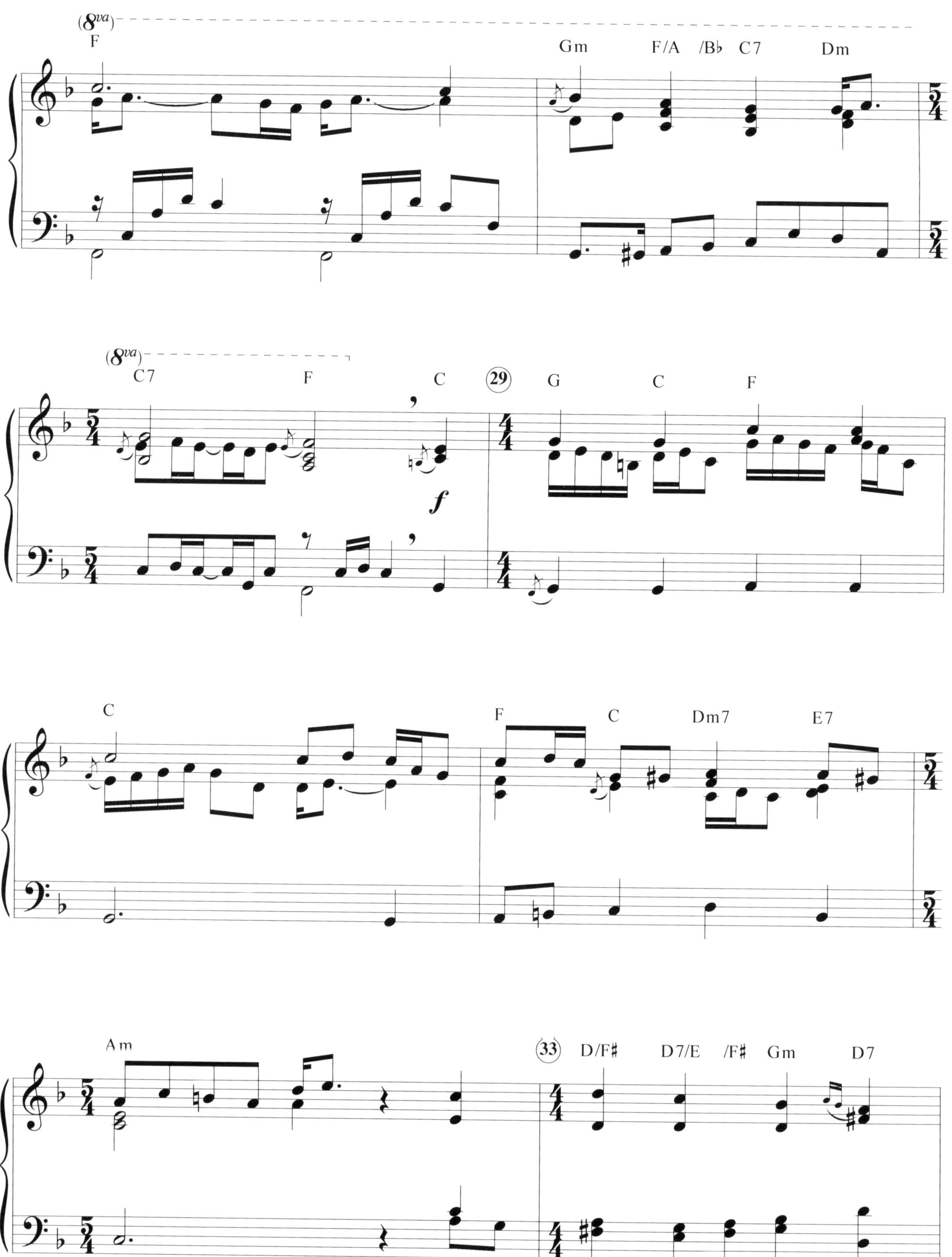
(8va)
F
Gm
F/A
/B♭
C7
Dm
C7
F
C
29
G
C
F
f
C
F
C
Dm7
E7
Am
33
D/F♯
D7/E
/F♯
Gm
D7

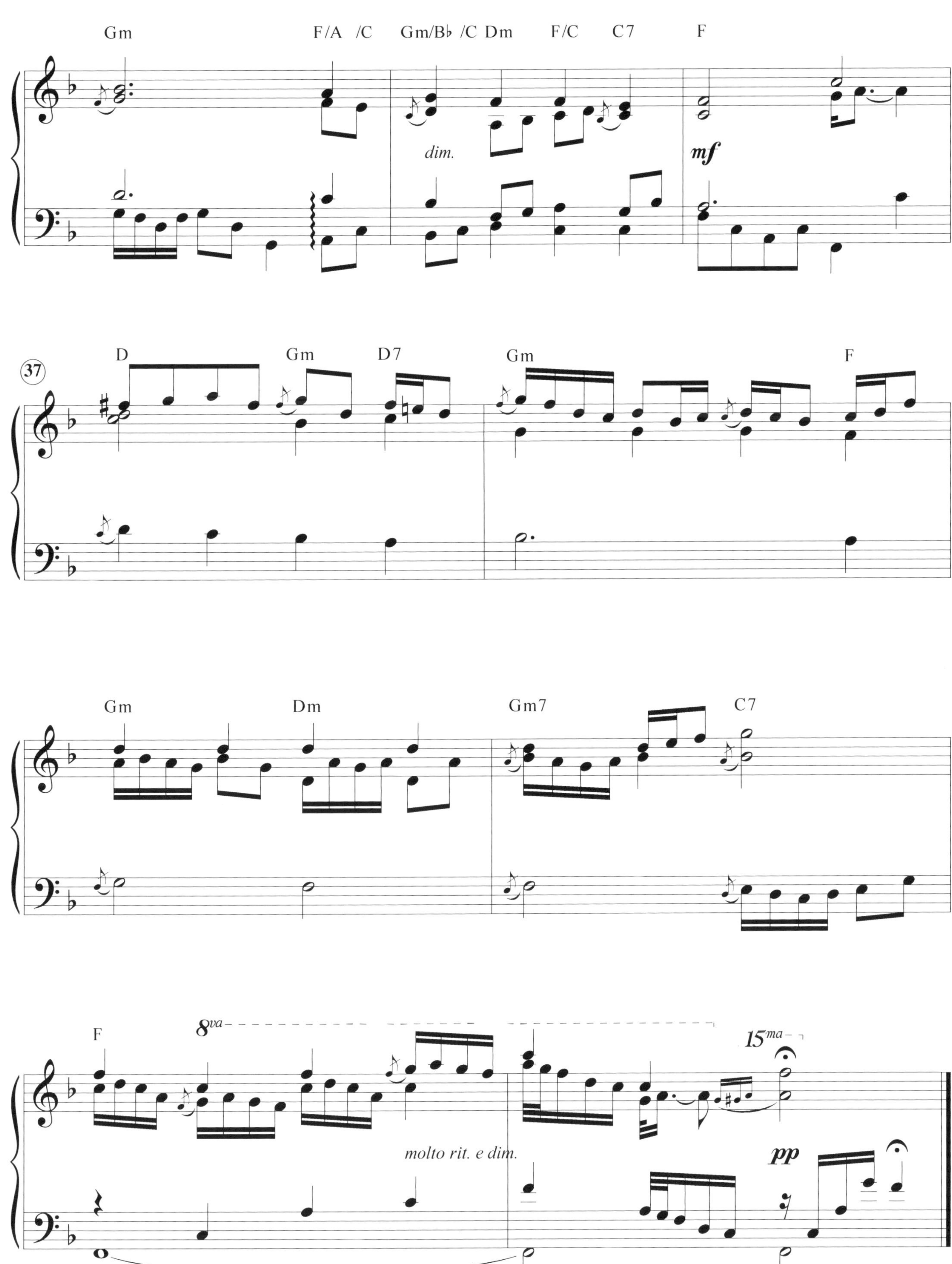
Gm
F/A /C
Gm/B♭ /C Dm
F/C
C7
F
dim.
mf
37
D
Gm
D7
Gm
F
Gm
Dm
Gm7
C7
F
8va
15ma
molto rit. e dim.
pp

Rejoice, Ye Pure In Heart

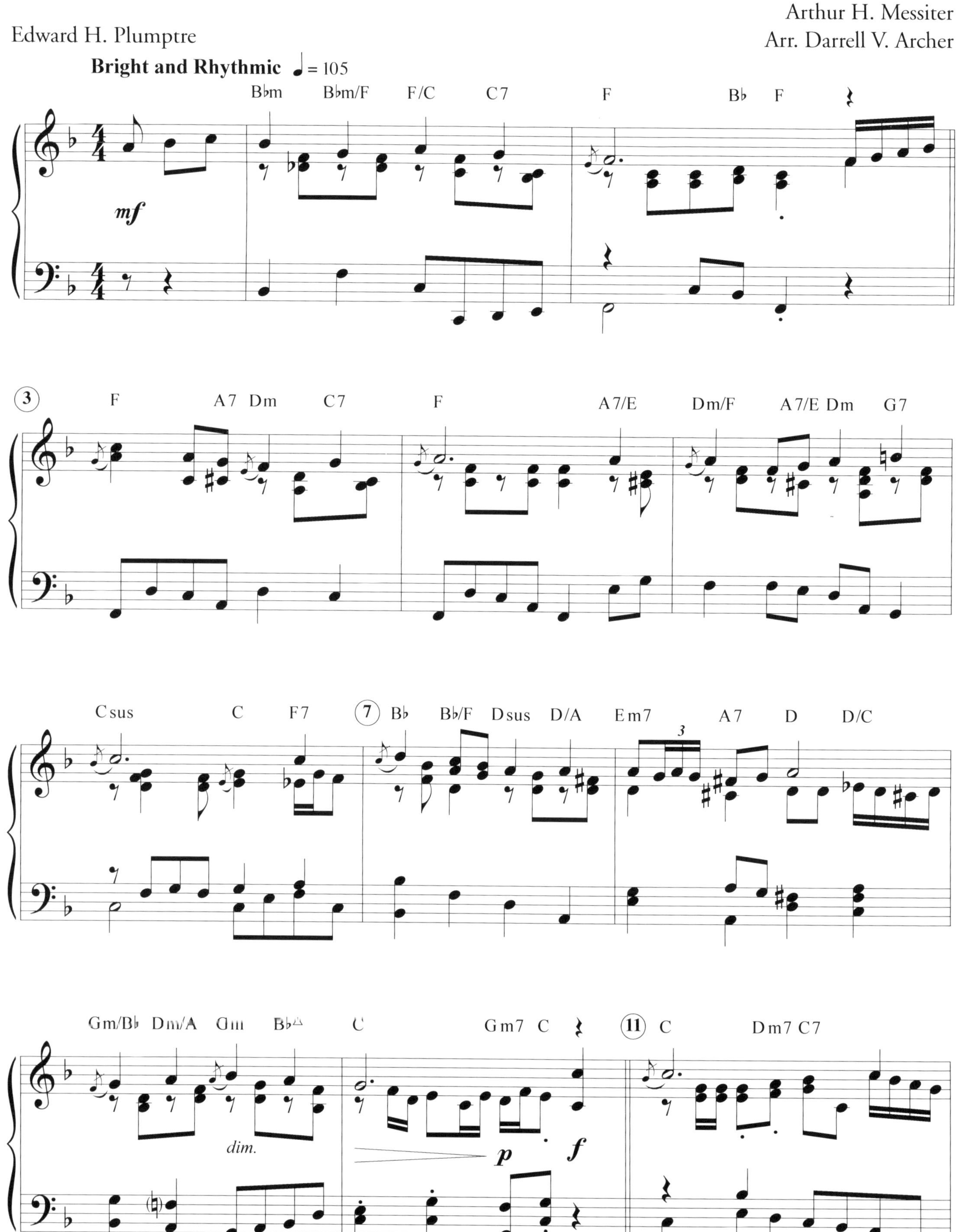

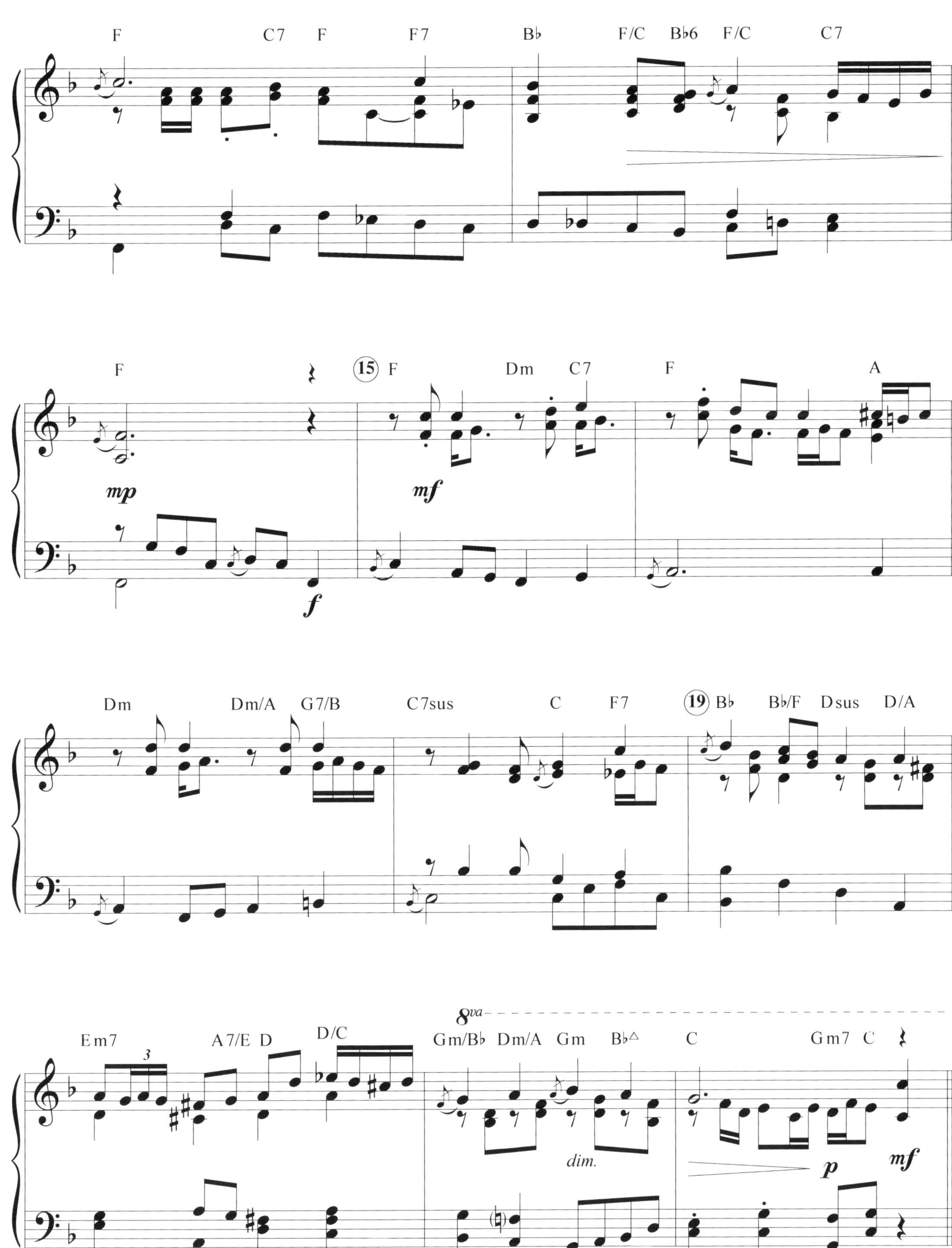
F C7 F F7 B♭ F/C B♭6 F/C C7
F 15 F Dm C7 F A
mp mf f
Dm Dm/A G7/B C7sus C F7 19 B♭ B♭/F Dsus D/A
Em7 A7/E D D/C Gm/B♭ Dm/A Gm B♭△ C Gm7 C
8va
3
dim. p mf

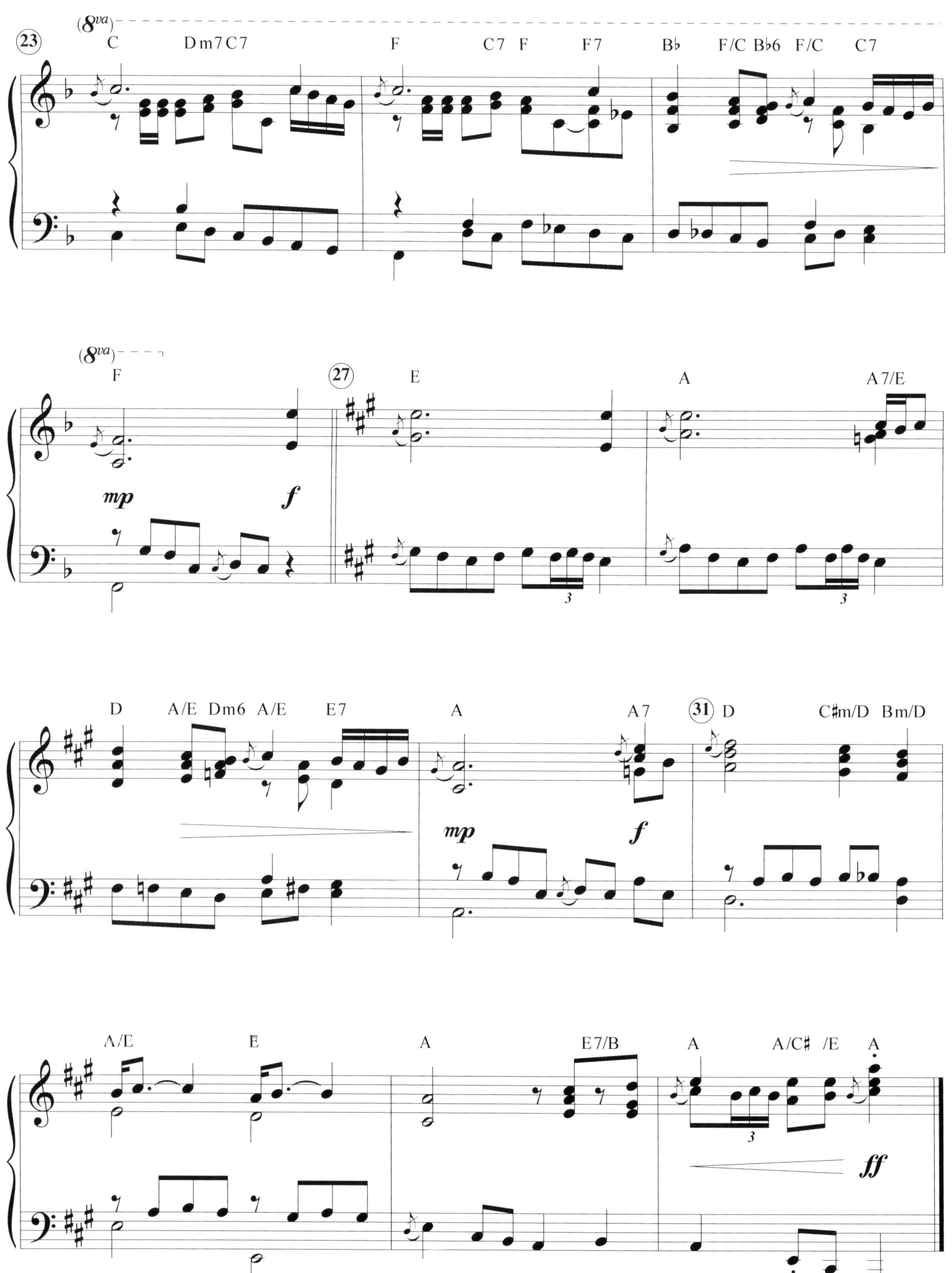
(8va)
23
C
Dm7 C7
F
C7
F
F7
B♭
F/C
B♭6
F/C
C7
(8va)
F
mp
f
27
E
A
A7/E
D
A/E
Dm6
A/E
E7
A
mp
A7
f
31
D
C♯m/D
Bm/D
A/E
E
A
E7/B
A
A/C♯
/E
A
ff

We Gather Together

Netherland Folk Tune
Arr. Darrell V. Archer

Adrianus Valerius

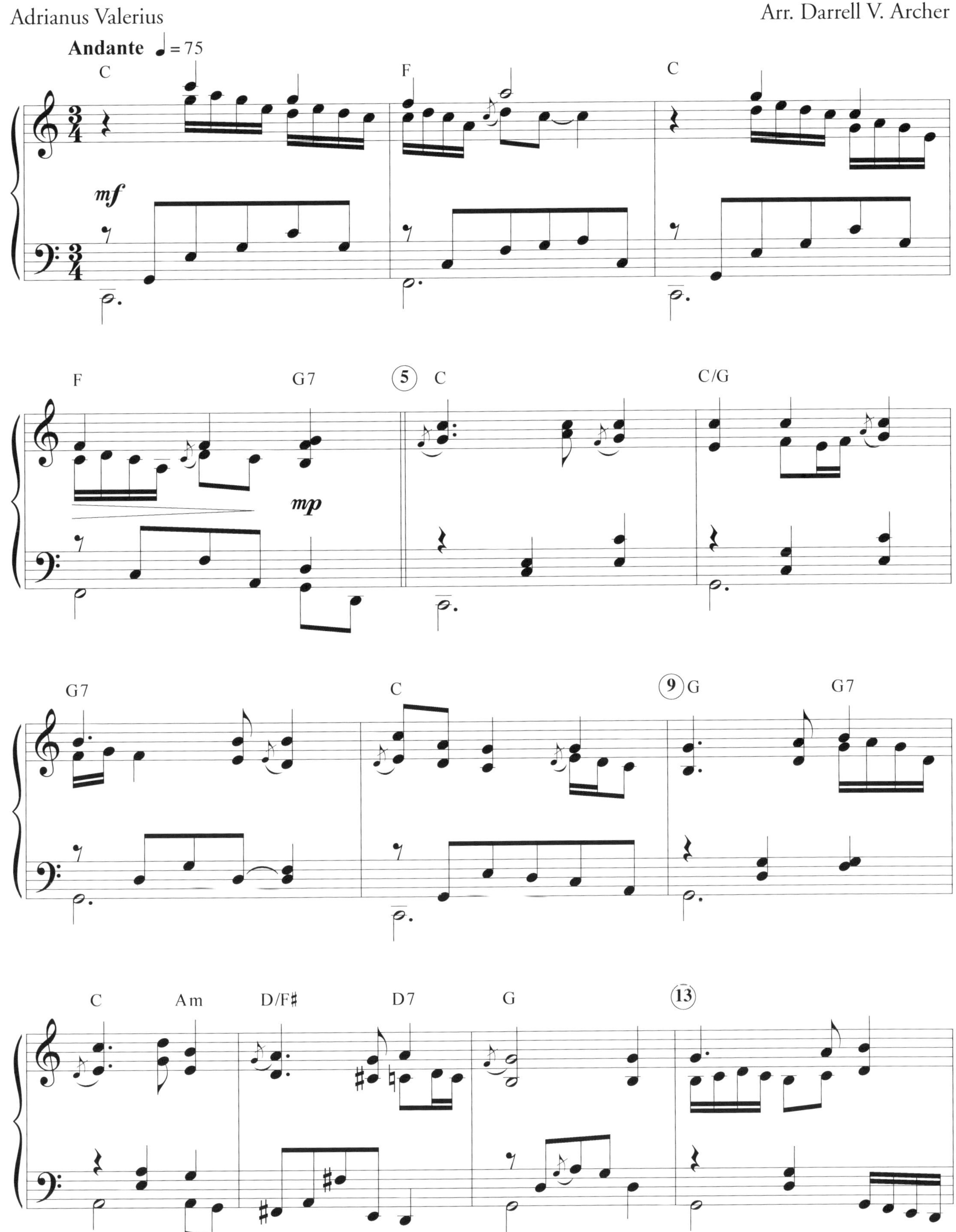

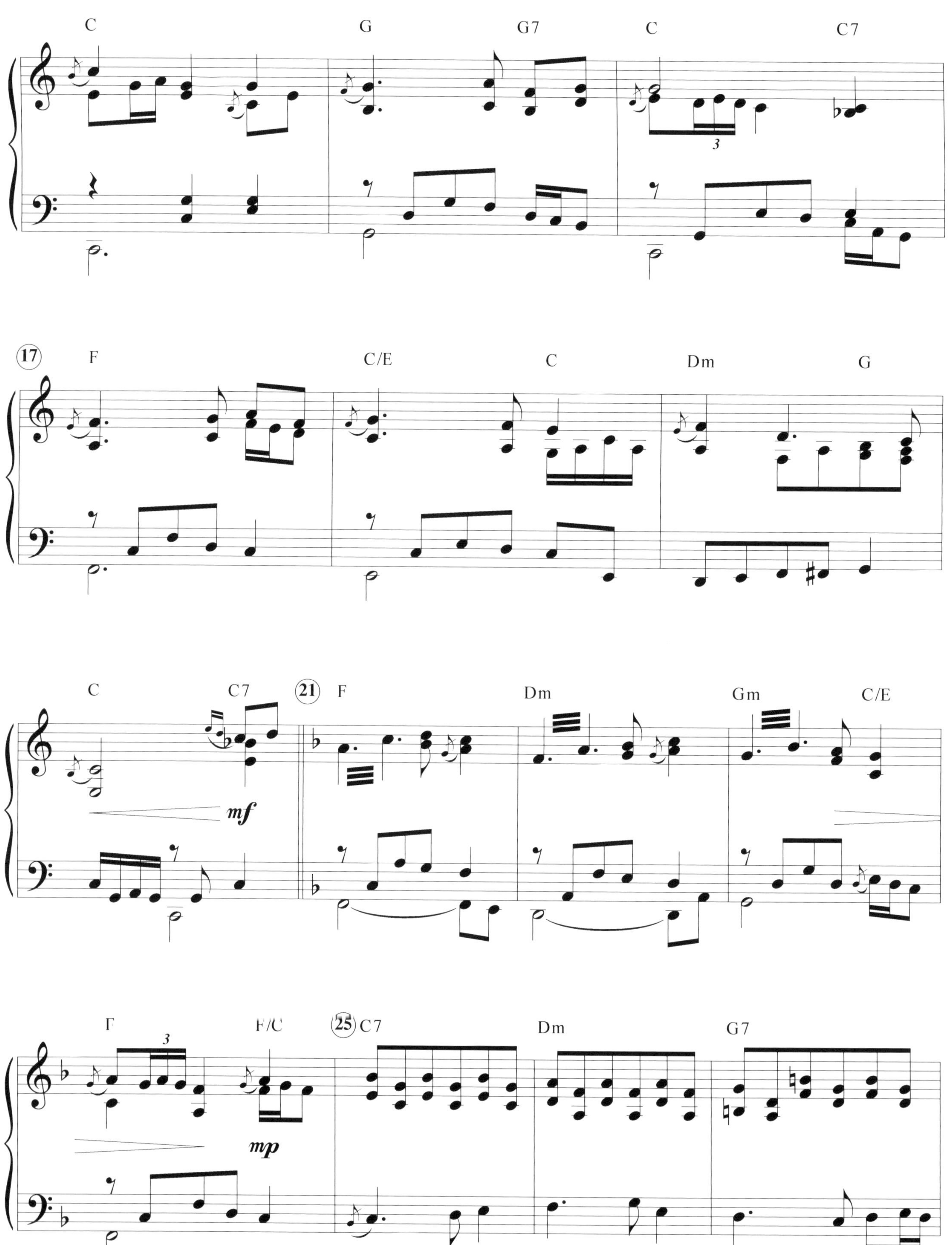
C
G
G7
C
C7
3
17
F
C/E
C
Dm
G
C
C7
mf
21
F
Dm
Gm
C/E
3
F/C
mp
25
C7
Dm
G7

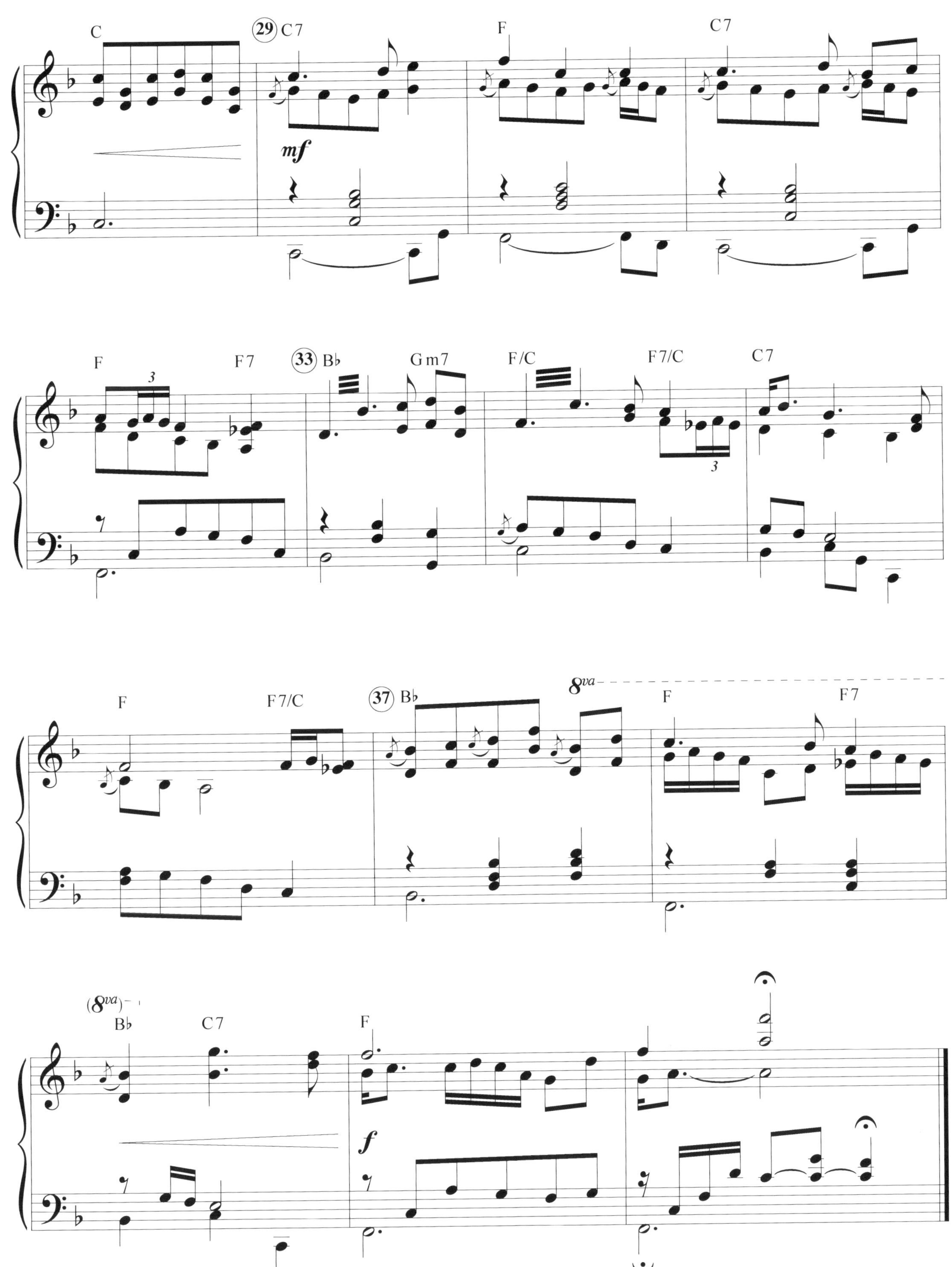
C
29
C7
F
C7
mf
F
F7
33
B♭
Gm7
F/C
F7/C
C7
3
3
F
F7/C
37
B♭
8va
F
F7
(8va)
B♭
C7
F
f

Other Mel Bay Sacred Piano Books

10 Gospel Favorites for Piano Solo (Archer)

12 Spirituals for Piano Solo (Gail Smith)

A Classic Christmas for Piano (Gail Smith)

A Country Piano Christmas (Archer)

Carols from Around the World (Archer)

Christian Classics for Piano Solo (Gail Smith)

Christmas Carols for Easy Piano (Benedict)

Christmas Carols for Piano Made Easy (Gail Smith)

Classical Piano for Worship Settings (Gail Smith)

Complete Church Pianist (Gail Smith)

Country Gospel Piano Solos (Gail Smith)

Country Piano Easter Celebration (Archer)

Easy Piano Solos for Worship (Shirley)

Easy Way Christmas Song Folio/Piano (S. Banks)

English Carols for Piano Solo (Gail Smith)

Favorite Hymns for Piano Solo (T. Price)

Favorite Hymns to Play for Piano (Leytham)

Gospel Piano Made Easy (Gail Smith)

Hymns Made Easy for Piano Book 1 (Gail Smith)

Hymns Made Easy for Piano Book 2 (Gail Smith)

Hymns Made Easy for Piano Book 3 (Gail Smith)

If Snowmen Could Make Music (Benedict)

Music is for Everyone Christmas Book Level 1: For Young Children (Gilbert)

Old-Time Gospel Piano (Cummings/Whitmire)

Praise Piano Made Easy (Gail Smith)

Preludes and Offertories for Piano Solo (Gail Smith)

Southern Gospel Piano - Blessed Quietness/Songs of Comfort (Archer)

Southern Gospel Piano - Land of Rest/Songs of Eternity (Archer)

Southern Gospel Piano - Devotion (Archer)

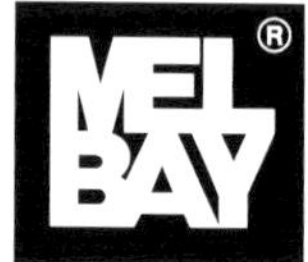

Southern Gospel Piano - Songs of Faith (Archer)

Southern Gospel Piano - Lyrical Gospel (Archer)

Wedding Music for Piano (T. Price)

WWW.MELBAY.COM